# PAUL, A TROPHY
# OF
# GOD'S GRACE

## Moses C. Onwubiko

# PAUL, A TROPHY
# OF
# GOD'S GRACE

## Moses C. Onwubiko

*NOTE: This book is the second in a series on grace. We recommend that you read the first one, <u>Overview of God's Grace</u>, before reading this book.*

# A SCROLL OF
# SOUND BIBLE TEACHING

*Buy Truth, and do not sell it.*

(Proverbs 23:23a)

Are you are aware that sound Bible teaching is a precious and priceless piece of spiritual jewelry? Indeed, Church history has shown the difficulties in obtaining it. Never has that been more true than in modern day Christianity! So, when God from His oasis of grace leads us to the pearls of truth in His infallible and inerrant Word, we ought to cherish them without reserve. The Bible is the treasure box that holds our capacity to enjoy abundant life, maximum happiness in life, friendship, marriage, and business, as well as the source of unprecedented blessing for today and tomorrow. Therefore, "buy truth" by staying grounded in the Word because truth "...is better than jewels, and all desirable things cannot compare with her." (Proverbs 8:11)

TRUTH: "For you are not under law but under GRACE."
(Romans 6:14a)

# ACKNOWLEDGEMENTS

May I seize this moment to express my deepest appreciation to the board members of Grace Evangelistic Ministries and to the associates and churches who are partners with us in God's service. Your financial and prayer support is, indeed, yielding fruit for the glory of our Almighty God. Your commitment and dedication to our Lord's work is beyond human calculation!

My sublime gratitude goes to Colonel R. B. Thieme, Jr., for his faithful communication of sound Bible doctrine. Colonel Thieme is a prolific author, who possesses a noteworthy command of the original languages of Hebrew, Greek, and Aramaic. For his perseverance on behalf of our Savior and His Word, I give unending thanks.

I am also profoundly grateful for the accurate systematic teaching of the late president and founder of Dallas Theological Seminary, Dr. Lewis Sperry Chafer, whose work helped uncover the Truth of the Church Age.

To crown my gratitude, my standing ovation goes to my best Friend, the King of kings, Lord of lords, the bright Morning Star, my eternal Lord and Savior, Jesus Christ. His efficacious sacrifice on the Cross two thousand years ago made it possible for me to communicate the Word of God today in this book.

# OPEN INVITATION TO THE UNBELIEVER

The information in this book can't benefit you unless you are born again, that is born spiritually. The good news is that you can be born again into God's family at this very moment!

When our Lord Jesus Christ was hanging on the Cross, He had you personally on His mind. No sin has ever been committed, no matter how horrible, that wasn't poured out on Jesus Christ on the Cross and judged. (I Peter 2:24) As the God-Man, Jesus Christ endured all afflictions, insults, and pain so that He might provide eternal life for you. The issue now is: Do you believe His payment for your sins was enough for your salvation?

Every good person has sinned and fallen short of God's perfect righteousness. God condemns everyone. (Romans 3:23) Therefore, both the good and the bad need a Savior. Regardless of how good you think you have been or how sinful you know you have been or how terribly you have failed in the past, you can begin a new life as a member of God's family right now. How? Simply by silently telling God the Father that you are believing in His Son Jesus Christ as your personal Savior. The very second you put your trust in the Lord Jesus Christ, you automatically become a member of God's family! Jesus Christ Himself said,

*Unless you believe that I am He* [the Christ—your Savior], *you shall die in your sins.* (John 8:24b)

The issue is faith alone in Christ alone.

*For you have been saved by grace through faith, and this* [salvation] *is not from yourselves. It is a gift from God, not as a result of human works lest any man should boast.* (Ephesians 2:8-9)

*For God loved the world so much that He gave His Son, the uniquely born One, so that anyone who believes in Him will never perish but have eternal life.* (John 3:16)

Will you believe in Him now? Faith alone in Christ alone is the only way to have eternal life. You may wish to pause now and believe in the Lord Jesus Christ. If you have believed in Him as your personal Savior, then continue to read.

# TO THE BELIEVER

Because you are a member of God's family through faith alone in Christ alone, your sins have become a family matter. In order to understand and benefit from reading this book, God the Holy Spirit must control your soul; however, the Holy Spirit can't control your soul if you have any unconfessed sin in your life.

*If we acknowledge our sins, He* [God the Father] *is faithful and righteous to forgive us our sins and to purify us from all wrongdoing.* (I John 1:9)

In confession, which is the acknowledgement of your sins directly to God, not to others, you, the sinner, come to a common agreement with God on the fact that your negative thought, word, or action was a sin. God has already condemned it as sin, and He expects you to admit to Him that it is sin. God has provided confession to Himself as the only means of being restored to a proper relationship with Him after you sin. As with salvation, restoration to fellowship with God is based on grace alone and not on your works.

When you have no unconfessed sin in your life, the Holy Spirit is no longer quenched or grieved; thus you are once again restored to fellowship with God and also controlled by the Holy Spirit. This is true spirituality.

*Now in the privacy of your soul, you should pause and acknowledge any unconfessed sin(s) to God the Father so that the Holy Spirit can make the doctrines in this book clear and effective in your life.*

# MY PRAYER FOR THE READER

*Dear Heavenly Father,*

*Father, I pray for those who will read this book, that their minds may be fully enlightened with regard to Your unfathomable, unparalleled, immeasurable, and matchless grace. I humbly ask that their inner eyes be opened to behold "how wide and long and high and deep" is Your unchanging grace toward the entire human race. May their understanding of this doctrine serve as a link to other biblical doctrines, such as salvation by grace and the eternal security You ensure those who have personally trusted in the Lord Jesus Christ.*

*May Your children for whom this glimpse of Your grace is new enjoy a sense of relief at the end of this biblical exposition. And I ask that Your promise in John 8:32, which states, "You shall know the truth and the truth shall set you free," be fulfilled for those who approach this teaching in humility. May they be set free from the bondage of legalism.*

*Please help us to "grow in grace and in the knowledge of our Lord and Savior Jesus Christ." May we come to the point, like Paul, that our lifestyle is forever marked with grace.*

*Thank you, Father for answering this prayer, which is lifted up in the Name of the King of kings, Lord of lords, and our Savior Jesus Christ. Amen.*

# Paul, A Trophy of God's Grace

# INTRODUCTION

We will begin our introduction to this book with a Scriptural abstract from the Pauline epistle to believers in Ephesus. In describing the Christian walk, Paul asserted,

*Let all bitterness and wrath and anger and clamor and slander* [Greek: βλασφημια, *blasphemia* = denotes wounding one's reputation by evil reports] *be put away from you, along with all malice. And be kind to one another, tenderhearted, forgiving each other, just as God in Christ also has forgiven you. Therefore be imitators of God, as beloved children; walk in love* [display a mental attitude of grace] *just as Christ also loved you* [with an immeasurable and unselfish love], *and gave Himself up [as a substitute] for us, an offering and a sacrifice to God as a fragrant aroma.* (Ephesians 4:31-5:2a)

Paul did not become a grace-oriented believer over night. Because he devoted his entire life to studying and applying God's Word, he grew spiritually; and consequently grace-orientation sprung up like a lily of the valley.

The truth of the matter is that no believer can be classified as spiritually mature without a component of grace-orientation in the equation of his spiritual life. I consider the apostle Paul a perfect example of one whose life experiences give us great insight into the awesome grace of God.

You may be asking yourself, how could someone who attacked God viciously be the greatest apostle the world has ever known? Paul, through the Holy Spirit, accurately called himself the foremost of all sinners. (I Timothy 1:15) He knew that he was totally undeserving to be God's servant. He was acutely aware that everything he had was a by-product of God's grace. When he zeroed in on his spiritual life with its many successes, he humbly said,

*For I am the least of the apostles* [a nobody, 2 Corinthians 12:11c], *who is not fit* [Greek: πικινοφ, *hikanos* = unworthy] *to be called an apostle, because I persecuted the church of God. But <u>by the grace of God I am what I am, and His grace toward me did not prove vain; but I labored even more than all of them* [other apostles], *yet not I, but the grace of God with me</u>.* (I Corinthians 15:9-10)

It's intriguing to know that through the infallible Word of God, we have the privilege of taking a spiritual tour into the chambers of the soul of the greatest apostle the world has ever known. Through Paul, we have a first hand glimpse into God's grace in action.

1

In the course of our study, we will see God in His matchless grace save Paul, the most arrogant unbeliever to ever emerge from a woman's womb! In the eyes of human viewpoint, he was unsaveable, but in God's viewpoint, iced with His grace, Paul, in the very second he put his faith in Christ, was snatched out of Satan's domain of darkness, instantly and eternally cemented into union with Christ, and blessed with every spiritual blessing in the heavenly places in Christ. (Ephesians 1:3) That was just the start. He then was commissioned to be the custodian of Church Age doctrine. Yes, you read it correctly! God chose the worst of all sinners to learn and teach the mystery doctrines of the Church Age.

Paul left the legacy of a lifestyle soaked in the ocean of God's unchanging grace. He challenged us to imitate God. Is that doable? He believed so, but only under the influence of God the Holy Spirit and with a soul piled high with God's Word. He knew that none of us would ever be perfect; nonetheless, as we renew our thinking daily with God's thinking as revealed in the Scriptures, we can come very close to living the life of Christ.

In the pages to come, you will see the apostle Paul, a trophy of God's grace, making grace the chief cornerstone of his gospel message and Biblical exposition of God's Word. He understood God's grace more than anyone in all Scripture. Not only did he have a grip on the subject, but also his thinking, lifestyle, and rapport with others were seasoned with the aroma of God's grace. We are now poised to dive into the sea of God's grace from which Paul received his trophy of grace.

# CHAPTER ONE
## PAUL'S HISTORICAL BACKGROUND

Tarsus, Paul's birthplace, was a Roman city located at the northeast corner of the Mediterranean Sea in the province of Cilicia and was a center for trade and learning in ancient times. (Acts 21:39) Many date Paul's birth a few years after Christ's. Paul was born a Jew of the tribe of Benjamin. (Philippians 3:5) When Paul was a small child, his family moved to Jerusalem.

From birth, Paul held dual citizenship for Israel and Rome. His Jewish name was Saul. The common notion that the name Paul was assigned at his conversion is incorrect. Paul was simply his Roman name. (Acts 13:9)

Through the grace of God, Paul received all of the benefits of being a Roman citizen, including special status and protections throughout the vast Roman Empire. In the Acts of the Apostles, Luke gave us insight into some of these privileges:

- FLOGGING: Commonly, in the Roman provinces, non-citizens who had been accused of a crime were flogged. In this way, the truth or a desperate confession could often be obtained before courtroom interrogation began. This technique was prohibited if the accused was a Roman citizen. In Acts 22:24-28, we read:

> ... the commander ordered him [Paul] to be brought into the barracks, stating that he should be examined by scourging so that he might find out the reason why they [those in the Jerusalem mob] were shouting against him that way. But when they stretched him out with thongs, Paul said to the centurion, who was standing by, 'Is it lawful for you to scourge a man who is a Roman and uncondemned?' When the centurion heard this, he went to the commander and told him, saying, 'What are you about to do? For this man is a Roman.' And the commander came and said to him, 'Tell me, are you a Roman?' And he said, 'Yes.' And the commander answered, 'I acquired this citizenship with a large sum of money.' And Paul said, 'But I was actually born a citizen.' (Acts 22:24-28)

On another occasion, Paul was inadvertently scourged and put in prison before his court appearance. We read again in Luke's account,

> Now, when they came, the chief magistrates sent their policemen, saying, 'Release those men.' And the jailer reported these words to Paul, saying, 'The chief magistrates have sent to release you. Therefore, come out now and go in peace.' But Paul said to them, 'They have beaten us in public without trial, men <u>who are</u>

3

*Romans, and have thrown us into prison; and now are they sending us away secretly? No, indeed!* [They must be out of their minds!] *But let them come themselves and bring us out.' And the policemen reported these words to the chief magistrates. They were afraid when they heard that they were Romans, and they came and appealed to them, and when they had brought them out, they kept begging them to leave the city.* (Acts 16:35-39)

Read that again. The chief magistrates, important and self-important leaders, left their courtrooms to come to the prison! Why? Paul was a Roman citizen.

POINT OF INTEREST: You will recall that our Lord was literally skinned alive during His sixth trial because He was not a Roman citizen. (John 19:1-3) His scourging was so severe that He became unrecognizable. (Isaiah 52:14)

- RESTRAINTS: Romans could not be handcuffed before they were convicted of a crime. In light of this law, Luke wrote,

  *Therefore, those who were about to examine him* [Paul], *immediately let go of him; and the commander also was afraid when he found out he was a Roman because he had put him in chains.* (Acts 22:29)

- RIGHT OF APPEAL: At one point, when Paul knew that he would not get a fair trial, he used the Roman right to appeal his case to the highest authority. In defiance of this Roman law, the chief priests wanted the Romans to hand Paul over to them. (Acts 25:15,16) They wanted him dead. Paul contended,

  *"If then I am a wrongdoer and have committed anything worthy of death, I do not refuse to die; but if none of those things is true of which these men accuse me, no one can hand me over to them. I appeal to Caesar!"* (Acts 25:11)

## PAUL'S TRAINING

The Jewish rabbinic custom was that every male learn a trade. In that way, no matter his pursuit in life, he had a marketable skill on which to depend. Our Lord learned carpentry; Paul learned tent making. (Acts 18:3) Paul often used this skill to support himself during his ministry.

Paul's training included much more than a trade. Historians agree that he was among the most educated men of his day. One professor suggests that he held the equivalent of our double-doctorate. Further, Paul developed a comprehensive understanding of Roman life, culture, and laws. Because he also trained under the tutelage of the foremost Jewish teacher of that time, Gamaliel, Paul was thoroughly grounded in Pharisaic Judaism, the strictest Jewish sect, abounding in man-made laws, rituals, mandates, and restrictions. (Acts 22:3; 26:4-5; Philippians 3:5)

After his conversion to Christianity on the road to Damascus, Paul developed his true theology. He independently sought God's guidance by withdrawing for a time into Arabia. (Galatians 1:17) Today, Arabia denotes the whole of a vast peninsula bordered by the Persian Gulf and the Red Sea, but in Paul's day Arabia was the desert region immediately east and south of Palestine inhabited by the Nabataeans. Some writers picture Paul traveling as far south as Mount Sinai, but it is unlikely that he took such a long journey. (Galatians 4:25)

Most agree that his trip to Arabia provided time for him to commune with the Lord Jesus Christ, whose Church he had so vigorously persecuted up to that time. Very quickly, under the tutelage of Christ Himself, Paul developed a keen sense of his mission and a profound understanding of Church Age doctrines.

After Paul returned to Damascus, three years passed before he met Peter and James in Jerusalem. (1 Galatians 18:19) With a brilliant mind, a thorough command of theology, and an ever-advancing love for God, Paul stood above his peers in many matters.

## GOD'S PROVIDENTIAL PURPOSE

The letters of Paul make it apparent that the Holy Spirit used Paul's broad knowledge of the history and culture of the Greeks, Romans, and Hebrews, and his mastery of Old Testament Scriptures and doctrines, to powerfully disseminate Church Age truths. Paul was providentially prepared to lead the missionary expansion of early Christianity.

PRINCIPLE: God uses prepared men. In Paul's case his preparation was unwitting. His training came as a grace package!

Have you realized yet that God uses your background for His own purposes?

Sometimes, a person is thoroughly trained in a secular field only to discover that he has a spiritual communication gift. For example, an engineer might realize he has the gift of pastor-teacher. *We* might ask, "Why waste all that time and money becoming an engineer if that training isn't relevant?" God never asks such questions. True, an engineer will essentially have to retrain to be properly prepared for advancing his congregation in their spiritual lives. He will have to study a huge body of ancient history in order to teach isagogically. He will have to digest the width and breadth of Bible doctrines in order to teach categorically. He will have to master the original languages of Scripture in order to teach exegetically. But the academic skills and the systematic thinking mastered in his engineer training are well suited to theological studies. God knew about his spiritual gift billions of years ago. He had a purpose in having him train to be an engineer.

PRINCIPLE: Nothing we do or learn is wasted unless we fail to prepare spiritually. Most tragically, the majority of those in pulpits today are totally ill-prepared to teach their congregations or glorify God.

Not everyone is called to the vigorous academic demands of the pastorate. Nonetheless, every believer has a spiritual gift, and that gift becomes fully functional as he advances in the unique spiritual life of the Church Age. His advance is predicated on the daily learning of Bible doctrine and its application to every circumstance of life. Of course, he can learn nothing without the filling of the Holy Spirit.

PRINCIPLE: The spiritual life is never what we can do *for* God. It is always what God can do *through* us.

PRINCIPLE: No matter our occupation or circumstances, God desires that we prepare, prepare, prepare. God only uses prepared believers.

Do you remember David, the shepherd son of Jesse? No one ever told him—and it is unlikely that he ever imagined—that some day he would become king of the Jews. Nevertheless, God began training him from an early age for the responsibilities of rulership. His training began as a shepherd when he learned the ingredients of leadership, patience, caring, and loving. More importantly, alone with his sheep, he was undistracted in learning and applying biblical principles, the central focus of his life.

We are trying to hammer down that wherever one finds himself—in the field of medicine, law, engineering, teaching, carpentry, housekeeping, or any other—when he has learned doctrine, God will one day use every bit of his life's experiences to further the course of His Kingdom.

## CHAPTER TWO
## SAUL'S PRE-SALVATION ENTHUSIASM TO SERVE GOD

Stephen was the first Christian martyr. As was our Lord, Stephen was accused of blasphemy and brought before the Jewish court, the Sanhedrin. Blasphemy was punishable by death. (Leviticus 24:16) In Acts 7, Luke records Stephen's testimony before the court in which he gave a synopsis of Israel's history of failure and rejection of Truth. The court's reaction to this condemnation was immediate and violent.

*And when they* [the Sanhedrin] *had driven him* [Stephen] *out of the city, they began stoning him, and the witnesses laid aside their robes at the feet of a young man named Saul.*[1] (Acts 7:58)

Saul did not merely stand by watching, but

*Saul was in hearty agreement* [present, active participle of the Greek word συνευδοκεω, *suneudokeo*—not a passive consent] *with putting him to death. And on that day, a great persecution began against the church in Jerusalem, and they were all scattered throughout the regions of Judea and Samaria, except the apostles. Some devout men buried Stephen and made loud lamentation over him. But Saul began ravaging the church, entering house after house and dragging off men and women; he would put them in prison.* (Acts 8:1-3)

In the following chapter we read,

*Now Saul, still breathing threats and murder against the disciples of the Lord, went to the high priest and asked for letters from him to the synagogues at Damascus so that if he found any belonging to the Way* [Christianity], *both men and women, he might bring them bound to Jerusalem.* (Acts 9:1-2)

Our purpose in recording Saul's disloyalty and violations of faith is to demonstrate the awesomeness of grace. Paul genuinely believed he was honoring God through his zealous persecution of what he considered a false Messiah and his anti-God followers.

PRINCIPLE: God never blesses our sincerity, only our correct application of His Word.

Colonel R. B. Thieme, Jr., of Berachah Church, has summarized the protocol plan of God for every believer with four axioms:

---

[1] We will use Saul to denote Paul before his conversion.

> A wrong thing done in a wrong way is wrong.
> A right thing done in a wrong way is wrong.
> A wrong thing done in a right way is wrong.
> Only a right thing done in a right way is right.

In the above verse, we readily note Saul's mental attitude, his enthusiasm to serve God. This desire to serve God was a right thing applied in a wrong way, which completely negated the rightness of his enthusiasm.

PRINCIPLE: When a conflict exists between a person's thoughts or feelings and the words of the Bible, the Bible is always correct.

PRINCIPLE: God has never needed anyone's help. Repeat, God does not need anyone's help—never has and never will—not then, not today, and not ever! Don't blaspheme God by adding anything to His perfect salvation work on the Cross.

## SAUL'S PERSECUTION OF THE CHURCH

Saul's self-righteousness was the driving power behind his enthusiasm to serve God by persecuting the Church. (Philippians 3:4-6) His pride in his qualifications as a Jew among Jews was arrogance, the same power that propels legalists, those that proffer lordship salvation, those who teach salvation by works, and the unprepared of every ilk.

Saul was absolutely confident that his every action was godly. He was totally positive but positively wrong. The rapid spread of Christianity intensified his flaming desire to remove all Christians from Jerusalem and beyond. Ironically, his persecution of the Church caused Christians to disperse around the world, thereby hastening the spread of Christianity.

PRINCIPLE: Grace causes God to change a disaster into a blessing.

Armed with an authorization from the high priest, Saul was hurrying to Damascus to purge the synagogues there of all Christians when our Lord appeared and said to him,

> "Saul, Saul, why are you persecuting Me . . . I am Jesus whom you are persecuting... " (Acts 9:4-5)

This indictment of Saul's pseudo-righteousness came straight from the Supreme Court of Heaven. Saul wasn't just persecuting, abusing, and torturing the saints, he was actually doing these things to Jesus Christ Himself because all believers are in union with Christ.

There, on the road to Damascus, Saul received his first lesson in Church Age doctrine, that of positional truth. At the moment of faith alone in Christ

8

alone, every believer is immediately placed in union with Christ. He is inseparable from Christ. This basic doctrine would become a prominent theme in all of Paul's letters. For example,

*Therefore if anyone is in Christ, he is a new creature.* (II Corinthians 5.17)

Let's take a quick inventory of Saul's status as a religious Jew. Arrogance skills (self-justification, self-deception, and self-absorption) distilled his self-righteousness into hatred. His hatred gave birth to rage, which manifested itself in persecution and torture. This persecution and torture targeted anyone who believed that Jesus was the Christ, the Messiah. Because every believer is in union with Christ, Saul's attacks were effectively directed at our Lord Himself.

Let's take a quiz. If you had been alive in Saul's day, what would you have determined he deserved for his brutal persecution of Christ? Would you have been willing to help God with his discipline?

Let's move on to this century. How often has your mastery of your own arrogance skills propelled you into hatred, rage, gossip, and/or maligning? How many times have you judged others? Not a pretty picture, is it? We all persecute Christ when we don't do a right thing in a right way. But as long as we are alive, we have the opportunity to reverse our negative mental attitude by the consistent intake of Bible doctrine.

PRINCIPLE: Only God knows how to judge because only God has all the facts!

And listen—if God can take a Saul, one of His major enemies, and use him as His foremost apostle, He can use you, too. How? Through the Bible doctrine you learn and apply to your life! Bible doctrine learned, believed, and stored in his soul was all Saul needed to become a true servant of Christ rather than a diligent worker of human good.

In Saul's thinking before he was saved, anyone who hung on a cross was not worthy of worship and certainly could not be the Messiah. (Galatians 3:13) The resurrected Christ gave Paul the doctrinal evidence that the curse of the Cross was necessary and temporary.

No, Christ will not personally appear to you as He did to Paul; but He has provided a pastor-teacher to teach you the Truth that will advance you in the spiritual life. Bible doctrine will enable you to keep your nose out of other people's business, to resist the temptation to judge anyone but yourself. You will be content to let God use and discipline others as He sees fit.

# CHAPTER THREE
## SAUL'S CONVERSION

We've examined the highlights of Saul's life and his high-powered enthusiasm to serve God. We've observed his enormous passion for God's service and his wrong use of it, which negated his passion. We are acutely aware that a right thing done in a wrong way is wrong. Saul's desire to serve God was a right thing, but his persecution of believers was wrong. Words are inadequate to express the intensity with which Saul tormented believers.

*So then, I thought to myself that I had to do many things hostile to the name of Jesus of Nazareth. And this is just what I did in Jerusalem. Not only did I lock many saints in prisons, having received authority from the chief priests, but also when they were being put to death, I cast my vote against them. And as I punished them often in all the synagogues, I tried to force them to blaspheme; and being furiously enraged at them, I kept pursuing them even to foreign cities.* (Acts 26:9-11)

Saul was a nightmare, a monster to the embryonic church! Wouldn't you expect the Lord to bring lightning upon such an opponent and send him straight to the Lake of Fire? Didn't he deserve to be separated from God for all eternity? But was he struck down or separated forever? No! Instead, he was assured of the crown of righteousness in eternity! Read it again: The crown of righteousness awaits the worst sinner of all time! That's grace!

In his last epistle, Paul (a.k.a. Saul), who had tortured the early Christians, wrote,

*For I am already being poured out as a drink offering, and the time of my departure* [to be with my Friend, Jesus Christ] *has come. I have fought the good fight, I have finished the course, I have kept the faith; in the future there is laid up for me the crown of righteousness, which the Lord, the righteous Judge, will award to me* [a depraved one in every sense of the word] *on that day, and not only to me but also to all* [who have also been graced out as believers] *who have loved His appearing.* (II Timothy 4:6-8)

We are examining the pivotal doctrine of Scripture, the doctrine of grace. Paul received grace in abundant and magnificent quantities—as do all believers! What transpired between the time Saul brought distress and suffering to the church and the time of his departure from earth? Grace, an unearned and unmerited favor done without expectation of return, freely given by the loving kindness of God to men, finding its only motivation in the bounty and free-heartedness of the Giver [i.e. God].

As we move forward in our study, we shall see Paul's understanding of grace reverse his thoughts, motives, and actions. The more he looked back to whom he had been before grace found him, the more he saw himself basking in the light of God's nature, grace. By the same token, the more you and I with our depraved natures understand grace, the more gratitude we'll have as graced-out citizens of Heaven with unmerited citizenship!

In the Supreme Court of Heaven, the righteousness of God condemned Saul of Tarsus for his atrocious and horrific attacks on the Church, the body of the second member of the Trinity, Jesus Christ. The justice of God demanded swift action, perhaps for Paul to be struck down with instant death and, thereby, separated from God for all eternity. But the Son of God pointed to the Cross of Calvary where the sins of Saul and everyone else were condemned by the righteousness of God, poured out on Christ, and judged by God's justice. The efficacious sacrifice of the Lamb of God, Jesus Christ, opened the grace gate wide. Saul walked through the gate, and became the object of God's infinite grace. That same gate stands wide open for you and me.

*And it came about that as he* [Saul] *journeyed, he was approaching Damascus* [where he hoped to torment more Christians], *and suddenly a light* [the Shekinah Glory of Christ] *from Heaven flashed around him; and he fell to the ground and heard a voice saying to him, "Saul, Saul, why are you persecuting Me?"* (Acts 9:3-4)

We will postpone our study of "Saul, Saul..." for a moment in order to rewrite this passage, "Legalistic believer, lordship salvation teacher, salvation by baptism advocate, salvation by works preacher, why are you persecuting Me?"

When any believer deviates from God's grace path, he becomes Christ's persecutor, an "enemy of the Cross of Christ." (Philippians 3:18) The solution for this kind of believer remains the same: He must name his sins to God the Father, agree with Him that what he thought, said, or did was, indeed, sin. (I John. 1:9) Then, he must begin to take in the Word of God under a grace-oriented pastor/teacher.

The conversion Saul experienced on the road to Damascus turned him to a lifestyle of grace. Our conversion should do likewise.

When Saul asked, "Who are you, Lord?" he received a reply that shook his world upside down: "I am Jesus whom you are persecuting." (Acts 9:5)

Saul was in shock. He froze instantly! For years, he had sincerely believed he was serving God when actually he had been attacking his Creator. He had been sincerely wrong. Saul beheld grace for the first time as he heard the Lord's instructions,

*"But get up and enter the city, and it shall be told you what you must do."* (Acts 9:6)

Apparently, Saul wasn't expecting to hear a testimony to God's grace. He was probably braced to hear, "Paul, you're toast!" Or "Because you have tormented Me, I will torment you. May worms eat you alive!" On the contrary, he heard the soft, sweet voice of grace from the Lord Jesus Christ saying, "Arise. You are with Me now."

## PRINCIPLES

- Saul's attack against both God and His believers stemmed from ignorance and self-righteous-polished arrogance. We may think we are serving God because someone is praising us or it "feels" right, never realizing that we are in opposition to God's will for our lives.
- Saul truly deserved cursing from God. He received blessing.
- The Lord Jesus Christ bypassed what Saul deserved and offered him an opportunity for regeneration. That's grace in action!
- Obviously, the events on the Damascus road were fresh in Paul's thoughts when he wrote to the Corinthians,

    *But by the grace of God I am what I am.* (I Corinthians 15:10a)

    He knew that were it not for God's grace, he would have been struck dead when Christ indicted him for persecuting His Church.
- Paul did not automatically become grace-oriented, but at his salvation, a building block was set in place. Reflect back to how miserable you were when Christ found you. Since then, have you ever failed God? Of course! Has God ever failed you? Absolutely not! Is the doctrine of grace beginning to register?

    *And he* [Paul] *was three days without sight, and neither ate nor drank.* (Acts 9:9)

The moment Saul was struck with blindness, he recognized his error and surrendered instantly to the omnipotence of the Lord Jesus Christ. Therefore, the three days of blindness became days of dealing with the Lord and soul-searching.

While Paul was cogitating on such amazing grace, the Lord called Ananias, a Church Age believer, to restore Paul's sight and reveal the divine commission to him. (Acts 9:11-12) At first, Ananias refused because of Paul's evil reputation. (Acts 9:13-14)

*But the Lord said to him, "Go, for he is a chosen instrument of Mine to bear My name before the gentiles and kings and the sons of Israel."* (Acts 9:15)

An ex-killer of Christians had become an *instrument of* God, not against God. That's *GRACE* capitalized, highlighted, italicized, and underlined!

Paul was saved by God while he was still spiritually blind, still depraved, and totally unable to undo his monstrous oppression against the Church. His salvation came solely as a result of his faith alone in Christ alone. Nothing in Scripture suggests that he invited Christ into his heart, made Christ Lord, or was baptized for his salvation.[2] True, Ananias baptized him but not for salvation; he was baptized because he was already saved.

In Acts, we witness a similar salvation by grace in Cornelius's house:

*"Of Him all the prophets bear witness that through His name* [Christ's essence and authority] *everyone who believes in Him receives forgiveness of sins." While Peter was still speaking these words* [the Gospel], *the Holy Spirit fell upon all those who were listening to the message* [because they believed]... [Peter added,] *"Surely no one can refuse the water for these* [new believers] *to be baptized who have* [already] *received the Holy Spirit just as we did* [on the Day of Pentecost], *can he?" Then he ordered them to be baptized in the name of Jesus Christ.* (Acts 10:43-44, 47-48)

Cornelius, his household, and guests believed in Christ as personal Savior and were instantly entered into union with Christ by means of the baptism of the Holy Spirit, not by water baptism.

Paul further confirmed that his and our salvation were totally grace when he said in Ephesians 2:8-9,

*For by grace you have been saved* [perfect tense in Greek: σωζω, sozo = saved at a point and remained saved forever] *through faith; and that not of yourselves; it is the gift of God, not as a result of works, that no one may boast.* (Ephesians 2:8-9)

Paul became well aware of the depraved condition he was in when grace found him. He had been working diligently for salvation by being the best killer of Christians and by obeying the Jewish oral tradition of laws, but to no avail. Works never avail salvation! No wonder Paul wrote,

*Nevertheless knowing that a man is not justified by the works of the Law but through faith* [alone] *in Christ Jesus, even we* [including himself] *have believed in Christ Jesus, that we may be justified by faith in Christ and not by the works of the Law; since by the works of the Law no flesh will be justified.* (Galatians 2:16)

---

[2] See *Biblical Doctrine of Salvation* by Moses C. Onwubiko.

13

Clearly, Paul's conversion was a perfect manifestation of God's grace. What have we learned from Paul's conversion?

- In Paul's helplessness, the Lord sent help. Paul didn't have to travel miles to Ananias. Rather, God brought Ananias to him. Similarly, the altar of salvation is brought to us. If you haven't already believed in Christ's work for you on the Cross, you can be saved anywhere at any time. You can even be saved right now if you so choose. Salvation is a matter of your choosing to believe in Christ, but all the work of salvation was completed by Christ on the Cross.
- The Lord is the One who seeks us in our depraved and lost state. He called Peter, Nathaniel, John, Zacchaeus, and (fill your name in here). He called Paul on his way to Damascus.

    *For the Son of Man has come to seek and to save that which was lost.* (Luke 19:10)

    Grace eliminates any suggestion of human effort for salvation.

- God does not deal with us on the basis of who we are, but rather on the basis of who and what He is.
- If God saved Paul, who callously slaughtered believers, and commissioned him to serve, anyone, regardless of his heinous sins, has the opportunity to be saved and serve God.
- No matter the sincerity of our service, if our works do not conform to God's plan, if they are not a right thing done in a right way, we are antagonistic to His plan. We are attacking the Lord.
- We should be very careful not to add to God's plan. Making an issue of baptism or making Christ Lord or any other gimmick as prerequisites for salvation are attacks against grace.

PRINCIPLE: God does not need our help. We desperately need His.

Throughout his epistles, Paul referred to his salvation and commission as divine works of grace. In his epistle to Timothy, we read,

*I thank Christ Jesus our Lord, who has strengthened me, because He considered me faithful, putting me into service even though I was formerly a blasphemer and a persecutor and violent aggressor. And yet I was shown mercy because I acted ignorantly in unbelief; and the grace of our Lord was more than abundant, with the faith and love which are found in Christ Jesus. It is a trustworthy statement, deserving full acceptance, that Christ Jesus came into the world to save sinners, among whom I am foremost of all.* (I Timothy 1:12-15)

What an inspiring statement of grace-orientation!

## GRACE-ORIENTATION

Grace-orientation is the mental attitude which a faithful believer develops over time. The more a believer exposes himself to sound Bible teaching on a regular basis, the more he sees his own powerlessness under the high-powered microscope of the infallible Word of God, and the more he strives to raise a Super Structure of grace in his soul through the utilization of grace assets, namely the power of the Holy Spirit and Bible doctrine.

To understand grace-orientation, we must first understand the doctrine of hamartiology (sin), which sheds light on who we are: Every member of the human race is born a depraved and lost sinner unable to save himself! Second, we must learn the doctrine of kenosis,[3] which opens our eyes to Christ's great love for mankind.

*That though He* [Christ Jesus] *was rich, yet for your sake He became poor, that you through His poverty might become rich.*
(II Corinthians 8:9)

*Although He* [Christ Jesus] *existed in the form of God, He did not regard equality with God a thing to be grasped, but emptied Himself, taking the form of a bond-servant, and being made in the likeness of men.* (Philippians 2:6-7)

Third, we must expose ourselves to the doctrine of soteriology,[4] in which we humbly behold the unique and unparalleled sufferings of Christ. As we slowly learn and believe the principles of the depravity of man, our understanding deepens; then, awe develops as we learn and understand the atoning work of Christ on the Cross, namely propitiation, justification, sanctification, redemption, and adoption. When we realize that we were spiritually dead, hopeless, helpless, and useless when God freely imputed His eternal life to us, then grace-thinking begins, and the Super Structure of grace in the soul is well on its way, all based on the foundation of salvation.

Fourth, another block of grace is added when it dawns on us that our work never impresses God. What does impress Him is what He does for and through man, especially Christ's sacrifice on the Cross. He wants us to understand and believe this basic doctrine so that we can continue advancing to the high ground of the spiritual life.

Step by slow step, as we learn and believe God's Word, we put the building blocks of spiritual growth in place. We begin to have an inkling of

---

[3].The doctrine of Kenosis states that Jesus Christ voluntarily restricted the use of His divine attributes in order to live among men with their limitations.
[4].Soteriology is the doctrine of salvation through the work of Jesus Christ of the Cross.

the price Christ paid to step out of His glory as God and put on humanity. We actually understand the mechanics of our salvation. We gain confidence through the power of the Holy Spirit and the Bible doctrine in our souls that we have a spiritual life that can take us to the high ground of maximum glorification of God.

Paul understood all these doctrines and beyond. Through his epistles, he communicated to us his understanding of the Church Age mysteries.

Christ's thinking is there in the Bible for us to learn. Only our positive volition is needed to open God's treasure chest of happiness, inner peace and tranquility, absolute confidence, and fearless strength.

# CHAPTER FOUR
## PAUL'S COMMISSION: GRACE ALL THE WAY

Paul's commission to preach among the Gentiles existed in the Lord's mind billions of years ago, long before either angelic or human history. Paul was by far the most educated man in his day, but his academic prowess had no bearing on his divine commission nor on the formation of the Super Structure of grace in his soul. He was appointed without a vote of his peers, without winning a contest, and without being best at something. God gave him his commission from his "mother's womb." (Galatians 1:15) God knew from before time that Paul would believe in Christ as his Savior and that teaching Church Age mysteries, especially to Gentiles, was his perfect spiritual gift.

### PRINCIPLES

- Paul's appointment was an issue in eternity past, far before God created the earth, much less gave Paul life; and, therefore, his appointment was totally unmerited. He could not have done anything to earn God's grace. Realization of the divine favor bestowed on him was the beginning of his grace thinking. Similarly, when you and I understand that we are in God's plan, in spite of our meddling or human works, we, too, begin to think in terms of God's grace.

- Paul's salvation and divine commission came to him at the pinnacle of his arrogance, when the cup of his self-righteousness and sin overflowed, when he repeatedly aimed to bring down the One who died for him. Paul, a master of the Mosaic Law, could barely believe God's grace. He knew from the Mosaic Law that any blasphemy against God was punishable by death. He had blasphemed and ridiculed God in abundance, and yet he not only remained alive but also received a divine commission! If anyone could echo the lyrics of the song "Amazing Grace," Paul would be at the front of the line.

> Amazing grace! How sweet the sound
> That saved a WRETCH like me!
> I once was LOST but now am FOUND,
> Was BLIND, but now I SEE.
> 'Tis grace that taught my heart to fear,
> And grace my fears relieved;
> How precious did that grace appear
> The hour when I first believed.

17

## PAUL'S EMOTION, FAILURE, AND GRACE RESCUE

We need to deviate from Paul's commission for a moment to examine some Biblical facts about emotion.

God is not emotional. He never has been and never will be. In my book *Biblical Doctrine of Salvation*, I taught the doctrine of the essence of God. One characteristic of God's essence is immutability.[5] God never changes, and He certainly doesn't have the mood swings that emotion leaves in its wake.

The only member of the Trinity with emotion was Christ in His human nature. He manifested emotion when He made His triumphal entry into Jerusalem. He wept for the city (Luke 19:41) and at the grave of Lazarus (John 11:35). Our Lord's emotions, however, were never sinful or self-pitying but always in response to a sad or glad situation.

A major drawback to feeling emotion is that its irrationality causes believers to steer off course of divine viewpoint. Even Paul, the greatest Church Age believer, allowed his emotions to override his thoughts, thus shipwrecking his spiritual life as we'll learn later.

PRINCIPLE: Emotion doesn't think, nor was it designed to think. It serves as a responder to a thought system designed by God.

Legitimate emotion includes grief, sorrow, joy, excitement, and the like. On the other hand, anger, bitterness, hatred, jealousy, guilt, worry, fear, self-pity, and depression characterize abnormal emotion.

We need to understand six major points about emotion:

- Emotion is designed to be an appreciator, a responder to rational thought.
- Emotion wanes easily as does any promise made under its influence.
- Emotion can hinder spiritual advance in God's plan.
- Emotion can cause a believer to drift from God's plan.
- Emotion is irrational and, thus, incapable of producing good decisions.
- Emotion is not worship of God.

*God is Spirit, and those who worship Him must worship in Spirit* [the filling of the Holy Spirit] *and Truth* [Bible doctrine, the thinking of Christ]. (John 4:24)

Now, we will examine an emotional decision which nearly shortened Paul's ministry. Powered by emotion, Paul made perhaps the greatest post-salvation mistake of his life, rejection of God's command to go to Rome, not Jerusalem. We are not studying Paul's emotional sin *per se* but rather God's grace in his life even when he failed so egregiously.

---

[5] Immutability means that God never changes. He is incapable of change. God's perfection will forever remain perfect.

18

God graciously sent Paul a series of divine warnings not to go to Jerusalem. (Acts 21) Because of Paul's negative volition to these divine warnings, the prophet Agabus

> took Paul's belt and bound his own feet and hands and said, "This is what the Holy Spirit says: 'In this way the Jews at Jerusalem will bind the man [Paul] who owns this belt and deliver him into the hands of the Gentiles.'" (Acts 21:11)

Paul rejected Agabus's accurate prophecy as well as the warnings of others, including the Holy Spirit, and defiantly went to Jerusalem. While in Jerusalem, James, the Lord's stepbrother, along with other out-of-fellowship believers gave Paul bad advice in the form of a human viewpoint solution. Because many Jews were upset that Paul wasn't observing Jewish traditions, Paul's friends strongly encouraged him to observe a ritual of the Mosaic Law, which he knew absolutely had been preceded by grace. Paul rationalized that by—just this once—forgetting grace and returning to an observance of Old Testament ritual, he could better influence those who opposed him for not keeping the law. (Acts 21:21-24)

Under emotional stimulation and the irrationality that accompanied it, Paul determined to undergo the Nazarite vow. He was entering the Temple for the last day of the ritual when a mob seized him and dragged him out to kill him. (Acts 21:31) While in the hands of this embittered religious mob, the Lord, whom he had disobeyed, came to his rescue by sending a Roman army commander and his men.

> And while they were seeking to kill him, a report came up to the commander of the Roman cohort [or battalion]....And at once he took along some soldiers and centurions, and ran down to them; and when they saw the commander and the soldiers, they stopped beating Paul. (Acts 21:31-32)

Paul came very close to death, but God in His infinite mercy and grace rescued him. Why? Because as he was being beaten almost to death, Paul recognized the enormity of his sins against God, and consequently, God preserved him from the sin unto death.

You may want to take a quiz. How many times have you failed God? I know that my failures probably outweigh yours; and yet, through my ups and downs, the grace of God has never let go of me. This is true of you also. Obviously, it was true of Paul.

## PRINCIPLES

- God never deals with us on the basis of who we are, rather on the basis of who and what He is, gracious and full of compassion. (Psalm 112:4)

Jacob, the grandson of Abraham, acknowledged that "God has dealt with me graciously." (Genesis 33:11) Here was a man who stole his brother's blessing (Genesis 27); and yet, God did not treat him in kind but bestowed grace on him in abundance.

- Before we were saved, we were rotten and spiritually decomposing in sin but nonetheless graced-out by the Master through faith alone in Christ alone. Paul put it this way:

    *And you were dead in your trespasses and sins....But God, being rich in mercy, because of His great* [unfailing] *love with which he loved us, even when we were dead in our transgressions, made us alive together with Christ. (By grace you have been saved).* (Ephesians 2:1,4-5)

Did you do anything to be saved? Definitely not! A hopeless, helpless, rotten person can do nothing to save himself. You were saved by faith alone in Christ alone. Everyone who has ever or will ever live is saved in one way only, faith alone in Christ alone, no additions, no corrections, no exceptions!

- After salvation, God continues to wrap us in grace. Too often, we fail God, but He has not failed us—not even once! He always welcomes us back with open arms. That's grace—never earned—never deserved.

- Whatever we are or could be is a matter of God's marvelous grace. Paul posed the question:

    *What do you have that you did not receive? But if you did receive it, why do you boast as if you had not received it?* (I Corinthians 4:7b)

- No believer has any reason to puff himself up, be it success in business, military, school, ministry, or whatever. In Paul's case, he was successful in everything he undertook. But when he inventoried his life, he humbly affirmed, *"But by the grace of God, I am what I am."* (I Corinthians 15:10a)

# CHAPTER FIVE
## PAUL'S DOCTRINAL ORIENTATION

We previously noted that Paul excelled beyond his peers and stood alone in his mastery of the Mosaic Law. He was even well ahead of the Rabbinical elite in religious matters.

However, great as Paul was in man's eyes, prior to his conversion, he was actually a stumbling block to the formation of the early church. Afterwards, he became the chief apostle. He delayed his missionary work to go to Saudi Arabia to spend most of his time learning from Jesus Christ Himself the doctrines of the Church Age and meditating on them. Here, he etched God's plan for the new dispensation into his thinking. Once enlightened and under the direction of the Holy Spirit, Paul wrote,

> *For I would have you know, brethren, that the gospel which was preached by me is not according to man. For I neither received it from man, nor was I taught it, but I received it through a revelation of Jesus Christ. For you have heard of my former manner of life in Judaism, how I used to persecute the church of God beyond measure and tried to destroy it; and I was advancing in Judaism beyond my contemporaries among my countrymen, being more extremely zealous for my ancestral traditions. But when He who had set me apart* (Greek: αφοριζω, *aphorizo* = select to office, set apart to serve. Romans 1:1), *even from my mother's womb, and called me through His <u>grace</u> was pleased to reveal His Son in me so that I might preach Him among the Gentiles, I did not immediately consult with flesh and blood* [literally, human beings], *nor did I go to Jerusalem to those who were apostles before me; but I went away to Arabia and returned once more to Damascus.* (Galatians 1:11-17)

Upon Paul's return from Arabia, the biblical principles he learned there from Christ became the focal point in Christendom. Still, you might ask, "How can I be certain that Paul was doctrinally oriented?" We will use a logical approach to answer this question. First, one cannot give what one does not have. That's just common sense and logic. Paul's epistles were printouts of the Bible doctrine engraved in his soul, the evidence that he was saturated with Church Age doctrine.

> *Now I rejoice in my sufferings for your sake, and in my flesh I do my share on behalf of His body* [the Church] *in the filling up of that which is lacking in Christ's afflictions. Of this church I was made a minister according to the stewardship from God bestowed on me for your benefit, that I might fully carry out* [explain fully] *the preaching of*

*the word of God, that is, the mystery* [Greek: μυστηριον, *musterion* = some sacred thing hidden or secret, only known by the revelation of God, i.e. Church Age doctrine) *which has been hidden from past ages and generations but has now been manifested* [Greek: φανεροω, *phaneroo* = to reveal) *to His saints.* (Colossians 1:24-26)

The more Paul, the custodian of the mystery doctrines of the Church Age, zoomed in on these unique doctrines (Colossians 1:25-29), the more grace-oriented his focus on life became. The thought of God the Father, Son, and Holy Spirit indwelling him at his lowest ebb was almost more than he could fathom. Think of it: The Creator indwelling His creation—every believer. If that thought doesn't humble you, nothing will. It boils down to this: When we have a handle on the Pauline epistles, master their teachings by studying under a sound Bible teacher, apply the principles consistently, sooner or later a mental attitude of grace will spring forth and blossom in our souls.

*And we proclaim Him, admonishing* [Greek: νουθετεω, *noutheteo* = to warn, instruct] *every man and teaching* [Greek: διδασκω, *didasko* = the thing aimed at when one teaches. *Didasko* means to shape the will of the one being taught by the communication of the knowledge of the word of God.] *every man with all wisdom* [Greek: σοφια, *sophia* = the knowledge of how to regulate one's relationship with God through the consistent, accurate application of His Word], *that we may present every man complete* [matured through Bible doctrine in the soul learned, believed, and applied] *in Christ. For this purpose also I labor, striving* [Greek: αγωνιζομαι, *agonizomai* = to wrestle, toil] *according to His power, which mightily works within me.* (Colossians 1:28-29)

Paul proclaimed that the Lord Jesus Christ was his personal Teacher in Arabia. In addition to the doctrines the Lord personally taught him, Paul put the Mosaic Law, which he knew better than anyone, under the microscope of Church Age doctrine, shedding light on the Law and the Prophets.

The Holy Spirit directed Paul to use specific Greek words in his writings, which indicated his doctrinal orientation. Four of these Greek words, all of which are found in Colossians 1:28-29 above, need further clarification.

1. *Noutheteo*, the first word, means to warn, instruct, or put something into someone else's mind. Before Paul could warn through the ministry of the Holy Spirit, he had to master Church Age doctrine himself. These truths had to be rooted in his own soul. He also had to consistently apply them to his life. In fact, he challenged Corinthian believers to watch his lifestyle and imitate him because he lived what he taught.

*I exhort you, therefore, to be imitators of me.* (I Corinthians 4:16)

2. *Didasko*, the second Greek word, also means to teach, but more than that, according to *The Lexical Aids to the New Testament* (a Greek dictionary), it means to shape the will of the one being taught. No one can infuse another's mind with his teachings unless the message he's teaching first impacted his own soul. Through the enabling power of the Holy Spirit, Paul was able to apply God's Truth to his life and, thus, reshaped his thinking to divine viewpoint.

3. *Sophia,* the third Greek word, means wisdom and describes the knowledge necessary to regulate one's relationship to God. In our context, wisdom means the accurate application of Bible Truths. When one is wise in the spiritual sense, he is said to be φρενιμοσ, *phrenimos,* one who is prudent with others and able to regulate circumstances. Paul was spiritually wise, and he hoped to impart that wisdom to all who would be taught his epistles. He turned the spotlight on himself when he wrote to the Ephesians,

> *Therefore, be careful how you walk* [live your life], *not as unwise men* [carnal believers or unbelievers] *but as wise, making the most of your time, because the days are* [short and] *evil.* (Ephesians 5:15-16)

He was giving the Ephesians a warning that he had already carefully considered himself, which underlines our premise that no one can impart what he does not have.

4. *Agonizomai,* the fourth Greek word, means to wrestle, strive, or toil. John recorded the Lord Jesus Christ using this word.

> *"My kingdom is not of this world. If My kingdom were of this world, then My servants would be fighting* [agonizomai] *so that I would not be handed over to the Jews; but as it is, My kingdom is not of this realm."* (John 18:36)

In light of these four Greek words, an important lesson emerges: For a believer to be an effective teacher of the Word of God, including the gospel, his message must first have made an impact in his own life. And, so it was with Paul—a model for his own preaching—and accomplished in the filling of the Holy Spirit to illuminate his mind with Truth.

POINT OF INFORMATION: Reaching such spiritual heights takes time!

We can learn only as much as our pastor-teacher knows. Since no pastor-teacher can teach beyond his own knowledge, years of academic preparation are vital. No short cut works in putting the nuts and bolts of Scripture together. It's not far-fetched to estimate that eight hours or more of diligent study and research are necessary to prepare one hour of accurate Bible teaching. Paul pointed this out when he said,

*I labor, striving according to His power* [the power of the Holy Spirit]. (Colossians 1:29)

A student of the Word may wonder, "Since Paul only wrote letters to the churches under the empowerment of the Holy Spirit, how do we know he really studied?" The Holy Spirit knew clearly that such questions would arise, and He supplied the answer in advance. In Luke's account we read,

*I know that after my departure savage wolves* [false teachers] *will come in among you, not sparing the flock; and from among your own selves men will arise, speaking perverse things, to draw away the disciples after them. Therefore, be on the alert* [watchful, vigilant, and of sober mind], *remembering that night and day for a period of three years I did not cease to admonish* [instruct] *each one with tears.* (Acts 20:29-31)

Paul taught the church at Ephesus for three solid years, though Luke only recorded Paul's farewell address. If all of Paul's teachings were put in print, we would need a ladder to read the Bible! The years and the number of times he taught each day in Ephesus were literal, not figurative. So if he taught two lessons a day, plus held a job, he would have had to spend most of his nights into the wee hours pouring over God's Word.

A good Bible teacher, in the course of his studies, should examine his life under the ministry of the Holy Spirit to see if his teaching affects him and, if so, to allow the doctrines to change his own life before presenting its truth to others. Here is Paul's way of saying it:

*You, therefore, who teach another, do you not teach yourself? You who preach that one should not steal, do you steal? You who say that one should not commit adultery, do you commit adultery? You who abhor idols, do you rob temples?* [Do you not exploit people by taking their money?] (Romans 2:21-23)

What came from Paul's mouth illustrated his life, so let's examine some verses at face value:

*I have coveted no one's silver or gold or clothes.* (Acts 20:33)

We are not sure how many ministers could say that today or how many believers for that matter. Paul went on to say,

*You yourselves know that these hands ministered to my own needs and to the men who were with me. In everything I showed you that by working hard in this manner you must help the weak* [the handicapped] *and remember the words of the Lord Jesus, that He Himself said, "It is more blessed to give than to receive."* (Acts 20:35)

24

When Paul had the option of exploiting those under his teaching by begging for money instead of using his trade as a tentmaker, he chose to work. When he had the choice of lying to get food or starving, he chose to starve. No wonder he could dogmatically state,

> *I have learned* [through rigorous studies of the Word of God and its correct application] *to be content in whatever circumstances I am.* [Through proper application of doctrine] *I know how to get along with humble means, and I also know how to live in prosperity; in any and every circumstance I have learned the secret of being filled and going hungry, both of having abundance and suffering need.*
> (Philippians 4:11-12)

We have demonstrated that Paul's thinking was saturated with doctrine. Why was his thinking divine rather than human viewpoint? Let's examine a few reasons.

- The doctrines of the Church Age were new and different from those of previous dispensations, thus Paul had to absorb it all in order to orient to the new era—the Church.
- Glorification of God was his objective. He knew that God is a God of precision and to serve God well, he needed to learn and apply the precise mystery doctrine to each circumstance he faced. You recall the principle that a right thing done in a wrong way is wrong. Today, many are serving God in a wrong way, which negates all service to the Lord and ends up as "wood, hay, and straw" (I Corinthians 3:11-15) at the Evaluation Seat of Jesus Christ (Romans 14:10). This was not the case with Paul. He strove to do a right thing in a right way.
- Paul wanted to know everything about the power behind Christ's celebratory victory on the Cross and His resurrection:

> *That I may know Him* [through intensive studies of the infallible Word of God] *and the power of His resurrection and the fellowship of His sufferings.* (Philippians 3:10a)

- Paul wanted to master and use the very assets Christ used in His humanity, namely the omnipotence of God's Word through the power of the filling of the Holy Spirit. Paul knew that Christ put His Father's Word above all else. In fact, Christ's last word on the Cross was *doctrine*:

> *Into Your hand I commit My spirit; You have ransomed* [Hebrew: *padah* = delivered, rescued] *Me, O Lord, God of Truth* [doctrine]. (Psalm 31:5)

Bible doctrine and its flawless application propelled the Lord Jesus Christ to triumphant victory at His first advent. They will bring us spiritual victory as well if we utilize them to the fullest.

- Paul desired divine guidance, joy, happiness, and peace.

*Your Word is a lamp* [Hebrew: *nerah* = a light, lamp, prosperity, instruction] *to my feet and light* [Hebrew: *owr* = illumination, enlightenment, happiness] *to my path.* (Psalm 119:105)

Jeremiah's words became Paul's own:

*Your words were found and I ate them* [believed and applied them], *and Your words became for me a joy* [maximum tranquility of the soul] *and the delight [satisfaction] of my heart* [soul]. (Jeremiah 15:16)

Do you want divine guidance, happiness, spiritual wealth, and peace? Then stay in touch with doctrine, today, tomorrow, the next day, and the day after that—all the way to your death.

- Paul had to make Church Age doctrine his own so he could run according to the rules that safeguard the dispensation of the Church.

*And also if anyone competes as an athlete, he does not win the prize unless he competes according to the rules.* (II Timothy 2:5)

When a believer ignores and/or rejects Church Age doctrine, he can't run according to its rules. Allow me to ask this vital question: Is your pastor-teacher feeding you the spiritual food necessary to advance to maximum glorification of God in this dispensation?

- Paul saturated his soul with Truth in order to advance to spiritual maturity and receive his rewards both on earth and in Heaven. He knew that the only way a believer can "grow in grace and in the knowledge of our Lord and Savior Jesus Christ" (II Peter 3:18) and be blessed in this life and forever after is through the day-by-day perception and consistent application of Bible Truths.

Upon departure from Ephesus, Paul told the believers there (and his words certainly apply to you and me),

*And now I commend you to God and to <u>the word of His grace</u>* [Bible doctrine], *which is able <u>to build you up</u>* [advance you to spiritual maturity] *and give you the inheritance* [rewards in time and in eternity] *among all those who are sanctified.* (Acts 20:32)

We can concretely conclude that apart from Bible doctrine permeating our souls, we can't have correct application; without correct application, spiritual maturity is a myth. Furthermore, without spiritual maturity, we have no capacity for life, friendship, marriage, or happiness—no capacity for superior blessings in time or in eternity.

## BIBLE DOCTRINE ALONE CAN'T ADVANCE ANYONE

Many Bible communicators stress the importance of learning Bible doctrine while at the same time neglecting to highlight and underline its *application*. No believer can advance one hundredth of a millimeter in his spiritual life without the perception and application of doctrine on a consistent, daily basis. We learn this vital principle in the Pauline epistles, which vividly declare that the test of Bible doctrine is in its application. In Paul's pastoral epistle to Timothy, he wrote,

> *Take pains with these things* [Paul's teaching of the mystery doctrines]; *be absorbed in them so that your* [spiritual] *progress may be evident* [visible] *to all. Pay close attention to yourself and to your teaching.* [See to it that your teachings are reflected in your lifestyle.] *Persevere in these things, for as you do this you will ensure salvation both for yourself and for those who hear you.* (I Timothy 4:15-16)

What does Paul mean by "you will ensure salvation both for yourself and for those who hear you?" For one thing, he was not talking about salvation from the Lake of Fire. Keep in mind that salvation is in three installments: Past, present, and future.

1.  SALVATION IN THE PAST: When a person anchors his faith alone in Christ alone, he is saved once and for all from eternal damnation. (Hebrews 10:14) Paul put it this way:

    > *Who has saved us and called us with a holy calling, not according to our works, but according to His own purpose and grace which was granted us in Christ Jesus from all eternity.* (II Timothy 1:9)

    God foresaw the salvation of every unbeliever in eternity past, billions of years ago, way before he could possibly have had anything to do with it, good or bad. If you have believed in Christ, your eternal salvation is irreversible history (Romans 11:29) because there is "no condemnation for those who are in [union with] Christ Jesus." (Romans 8:1)

2.  SALVATION IN THE PRESENT: Salvation in time means God delivers the believer through the power of the filling of the Holy Spirit and the power of a soul saturated with God's Truth. Every believer is responsible for learning and applying Bible doctrine to all circumstances. If he does so, God promises to deliver him from the sin unto death. Any believer who fails to use God's solutions walks precariously in harm's way and will ultimately suffer the sin unto death.

Salvation in time comes only to those who follow God's rules as set forth in the Bible, to those who do a right thing in a right way.

*For if you are living according to the flesh* [in carnality], *you must die* [the sin face-to-face with death]; *but if by* [the enabling power of] *the Holy Spirit you are putting to death the deeds of the body* [the sin nature], *you will live.* [You will be saved in time from the sin unto death.] (Romans 8:13)

3.  SALVATION IN THE FUTURE: In the final installment of salvation, God removes the believer from life and gives him his own resurrection body. (I Corinthians 15:51-57)

Concerning the importance of the application of Bible doctrine to salvation in time, the Lord Himself uttered these words:

*"Everyone who comes to Me and hears* [learns] *My words* [Bible doctrine] *and acts upon them* [applies them to his life], *I will show you whom he is like: He is like a man building a house, who dug deep and laid a foundation upon the rock; and when a flood rose, the torrent burst against that house and could not shake it because it had been well built. But the one who has heard and has not acted accordingly* [not applied the doctrine he learned] *is like a man who built a house upon the ground without any foundation; and the torrent burst against it and immediately it collapsed, and the ruin of that house was great."* (Luke 6:47-49)

The Lord's teaching on this point enveloped the principle that perception of Bible doctrine without its application is meaningless.

*"My mother and My brothers are these who hear the word of God and do* [apply] *it."* (Luke 8:21)

He further hammered home this crucial truth when a rude woman interrupted His teaching:

*And it came about while He said these things, one of the women in the crowd raised her voice and said to Him, "Blessed is the womb that bore You and the breast at which You nursed." But He* [the Lord Jesus Christ] *said, "On the contrary* [wrong!], *blessed* [happy] *are those who hear the word of God and observe* [Greek: φυλασσω, *phulasso* = guard, watch, apply] *it."* (Luke 11:27-28)

James, the stepbrother of our Lord Jesus Christ, put it this way:

*But prove yourselves doers of the Word and not merely hearers who delude themselves. For if anyone is a hearer of the Word and not a doer* [doesn't apply the doctrine he has learned], *he is like a man who looks*

*at his natural face in a mirror; and once he has looked at himself
and gone away, he has immediately forgotten what kind of person he
was. But one who looks intently at the perfect law* [sound Bible doctrine],
*the law of liberty, and abides by it* [Greek: παραμενω, *parameno* =
connotes both retention and application], *not having become a forgetful
hearer but an effectual doer, this man shall be blessed in what he
does.* (James 1:22-25)

It is important to reiterate that the doctrine in Paul's soul and his
perseverance in using it transformed his human viewpoint thinking to divine
viewpoint, causing him to become humble in his relationship with God and
others, preparing him to be a grace-oriented believer, propelling him to
spiritual maturity, and making his life precious both to elect angels and to
believers of the world.

### EXAMPLES OF THE CORRECT APPLICATION OF DOCTRINE

No two believers apply Bible doctrine in the same way, so we are going
to throw out random samplings of correct application:

- Suppose a believer becomes the victim of malicious gossip. He has one
  of two options; he can break fellowship with God by reacting in
  bitterness and seeking to get even with the mastermind of the gossip, or
  he can apply the doctrine of "leave all injustice in God's hand." Paul
  wrote:

  *Never pay back evil for evil... Never take your own revenge,
  beloved, but leave room for the wrath of God, for it is written* [in
  Deuteronomy 32:35], *"VENGEANCE IS MINE; I WILL REPAY
  SAYS THE LORD."* (Romans 12:17, 19)

- Suppose things fall apart in a believer's life. He can become panic-
  stricken about the future and immediately forfeit fellowship with God
  and lose the filling of the Holy Spirit and tranquility of soul, or he can
  relax and apply doctrine as Paul did.

  *And we know that God causes all things* [loss of loved ones, health,
  employment, wealth, etc.] *to work together for good to those <u>who love
  God</u>, to those who are called according to His purpose.*
  (Romans 8:28)

The believer can also find great comfort and hope in Job's application.
Remember, Job was under the severest testing and temptation
possible—straight from Satan himself, and yet he was able to proclaim,

  *"As for me, I know that my Redeemer lives."* (Job 19:25a)

- Suppose someone in a believer's immediate periphery (his husband, wife, child, or friend) does not conform to his standards. He can react (a symptom of immaturity) and scream against such blatantly wrong behavior, or he can reach into his soul and pull out virtuous love:

  *Love is patient; love is kind and is not jealous; love does not brag and is not arrogant, does not act unbecomingly; it does not seek its own, is not provoked, does not take into account a wrong suffered... Love never fails.* (I Corinthians 13:4-8a)

- Suppose a believer has an opportunity to become rich by the exploitation of others. He juggles the doctrine in his soul against the temptation of wealth and comes to the conclusion that any profit not directly from God is no profit after all!

  *It is the blessing of the Lord that makes rich, and He adds no sorrow to it.* (Proverbs 10:22)

- Suppose a believer is at a crossroad in his life. If he has stored an arsenal of doctrine in his soul, he doesn't fret. Rather, under the filling of the Holy Spirit, he waits on the Lord; and while waiting, he reminds himself,

  *For such is God, Our God forever and ever; He will guide us until death.* (Psalm 48:14)

  And he seriously concentrates on our Lord's words:

  *I will instruct [guide] you and teach you in the way which you should go; I will counsel you with My eye upon you.* (Psalm 32:8)

- Suppose the believer is in severe suffering. Like Job, he draws upon God's word in his soul.

  *Though He slay me, I will hope [have absolute confidence] in Him.* (Job 13:15)

  The suffering believer holds on, never retreating to self-pity but reaching the same conclusion as Job:

  *But He knows the way [Hebrew: derek: journey, course] I take; when He has tried me, I shall come forth as gold.* (Job 23:10)

In plain language, Job was saying, "God knows what I'm going through, and He knows how and when to get me out of it and make my life more splendid. After all, He alone can blend bad things with good things and come out with a product of intrinsic, lasting good."

As we ride the waves of our spiritual lives, we will face a multitude of tests. The Lord is glorified in our testing only when we utilize the same powers He used in His incarnation, the power of Bible doctrine stored in the soul ready for instant deployment and the power of the filling of the Holy Spirit. These divine assets are provided in grace and utilized in grace under the filling of the Holy Spirit. Without the filling of the Holy Spirit, application of Bible doctrine is impossible; therefore, acknowledge all sins to God the Father so that you can learn and apply His Word, and, thereby, glorify Him.

# CHAPTER SIX
## PAUL'S GRACE-ORIENTATION

We've examined Paul's doctrinal orientation. We've exegeted Colossians 1:24-26 and arrived at the conclusion that Paul's spiritual life was centered on the daily perception of the infallible Word of God. We noted that his lifestyle of daily study and application of Bible doctrine made his life precious to both believers of the world and elect angels. His doctrinal orientation caused him to develop a mental attitude of grace. Now we are poised to study Paul's grace-orientation.

We need to lay our basic groundwork. The first thing we need to know is that grace-orientation is a mental attitude, nothing more, nothing less. From the chambers of our souls come our actions, both in deeds and words.

*As a man thinks* [in his soul] *so he is.* (Proverbs 23:7)

To be precise, "You are what you think."

The second building block of grace-orientation is developed through the perception and application of the inerrant word of God. Consequently, a person's mental attitude falls into two categories: Arrogance and humility.

## ARROGANCE

Arrogant thinking is the most heinous sin of both human and angelic history. Ironically, believers by the millions are not aware that Satan is the author and master of arrogance. These believers forget or never knew that arrogance was the source of Satan's fall. (Isaiah 14:12-15; Ezekiel 28:18) Even more chilling, many believers have become his victims. Adam and Eve were his first victims.

*We* should be frightened of falling into the arrogance trap because God makes war against anyone who lives a lifestyle of arrogance. In the book of Proverbs, God's attitude and warning in regard to arrogance stands tall.

*Everyone who is proud in heart is an abomination* [Hebrew: *toebah* = abomination, loathsome, detestable thing] *to the Lord; assuredly, he* [the arrogant one] *will not be unpunished* [by the Supreme Court of Heaven]. (Proverbs 16:5)

You may ask, "How can I discern when my mental attitude is in the arrogant mode?" The answer can be summarized in a poetic expression:

*When you think that your own agenda is more important than God's, from the fountain of arrogance you drink.*
*When you think that Bible doctrine is secondary to anything else, up the hill of arrogance you climb.*

*When one iota of pride is in your thinking, down the path of self-destruction you walk.*

*When you think that you have something to prove to others, the goggles of arrogance you wear.*

*When self-approbation occupies your soul, the bell of arrogance you hear.*

*When power lust captivates your soul, on the high chair of arrogance you sit.*

*When you compete with other believers, in arrogance's danger zone you compete.*

*When you think that your success came through something you did, to the music of arrogance you dance.*

*When you venture to grab God's glory, in the bed of the sin-unto-death you sleep.*

*When you think that others cannot do without you, on the sinking ground you stand.*

*When you think that you are better than others, down the valley of arrogance you slide.*

*When people's praise inflates you, on the door of God's wrath you knock.*

*When you think that you have all the answers, in the room of darkness you wander.*

*When you stop learning from others, the wealth of knowledge you forgo.*

*When you think that you have arrived, at the door of the assembly of the dead you stand.*

The Bible is crystal clear about arrogance.

*God is opposed to the proud* [makes war against the arrogant believer], *but gives* [super] *grace to the humble.* (James 4:6b)

Undoubtedly, Paul was the epitome of arrogance before his salvation experience. Paul, then called Saul, heard the Gospel straight from the mouth of Stephen, an early Christian martyr, as he was being stoned to death, but Saul rejected salvation by faith. (Acts 7) Rather, in arrogance, he was consumed with high-powered anger to eliminate Christ's Name and any who identified with Him. (Acts 8)

Did Paul succumb to arrogance in his post-salvation life? Many think that just by being believers, they are shielded from Satan's disguised strategy to lure them into becoming arrogant. Such doctrinally ignorant believers should learn from Paul. Perhaps because he was still in spiritual babyhood or adolescence, Paul in arrogance decided to go to Jerusalem rather than to Rome as God commanded him. Subsequently, Paul was warned several times through the Holy Spirit not to go to Jerusalem. (Acts 21:4, 10-12)

> *Then Paul answered, "What are you doing, weeping and breaking my heart? For I am ready not only to be bound but even to die at Jerusalem for the name of the Lord Jesus."* (Acts 21:13)

Paul rationalized that his plan to go to Jerusalem would be more fruitful than the Lord's restriction on him not to set foot in Jerusalem. He decided he knew better than God! He piously declared he was ready to die for Jesus Christ—even though, as Paul knew, God's plan was to keep him alive. Because Paul was out of fellowship, not filled with the Holy Spirit, he would come close to dying the sin unto death as an enemy of Christ, not as His servant.

Paul's embrace of arrogant thinking nearly ended his life when the Jewish mob attacked him while he was in the Temple in Jerusalem. (Acts 21:27-30) But at the last moment of life, Paul confessed his arrogance to God the Father, and the Lord in His inexpressible grace rescued him. (Acts 21:31-33)

PRINCIPLE: God is faithful to deliver us if we acknowledge our sins to Him. No situation is too impossible for His grace.

Undebatably, Paul's grace-rescue was also a building block in his development of grace-orientation, but his lapse into arrogance was not without a price. God always keeps His word. Arrogance, wherever it rears its ugly head, shall not go unpunished. (Proverbs 16:5) Paul would spend most of the rest of his life in prison in Rome. Further, from that day forward, his suffering for Christ intensified. Through this suffering, laced with his constant focus on Christ, garnished with his daily perception and application of Bible doctrine, Paul erected a fortification of humility in his soul block-by-doctrinal-block.

## HUMILITY

Humility is the opposite of arrogance. Humility and arrogance are mutually exclusive. They cannot co-exist. Humility is a state of mind in which one regards himself as "Mr. Nobody of Any Significance" and easily and joyfully submits to any appointed authority.

Jesus Christ was the Pioneer of true humility. In His incarnation, He submitted unconditionally and unequivocally, even to the extent of death, to the authority and will of God the Father.

> *Who* [Jesus Christ] *although He existed in the form of God, did not regard equality with God a thing to be grasped* [Greek: αρπαγμοφ, *harpagmos* = robbery], *but emptied Himself, taking the form of a bond-*

*servant* [Greek: δουλοφ, *doulos* = a slave, one who is in a permanent relationship of servitude to another, his will altogether consumed in the will of the other], *and being made in the likeness of men. And being found in appearance as a man, He humbled Himself* [Greek: ταπεινοω, *tapeinoo* = to humble or bring low] *by becoming obedient to death, even death on a cross.* (Philippians 2:6-8)

Jesus Christ is equal to God the Father, yet He willingly, in perfect humility, subjugated Himself to the Father's will. The Scriptures have a bundle of information to prove that Jesus Christ is equal with the first Member of the Trinity, namely God the Father. One piece of evidence is in our context above. Also, in Hebrews we read that

*He* [Jesus Christ] *is the radiance of His* [God's] *glory and the exact representation of His nature.* (Hebrews 1:3a)

Jesus Christ, in the equality of His deity, could have said to God the Father, "Who do You think you are to give Me instructions? Do it yourself! After all, we are equal in essence." Such a statement, though correct, would have been arrogant. Thank God that our Savior didn't think such thoughts because arrogance would have ended any chance of our salvation! Much to our relief, He said,

*"A* [human] *body You* [God the Father] *have prepared for Me."* (Hebrews 10:5)

In addition, Christ affirmed,

*"My food is to do the will of Him who sent Me and to accomplish His work."* (John 4:34)

Instead of being pre-occupied with Himself, Christ was pre-occupied with the Father's plan. In light of His mission, His thinking was aligned perfectly with His Father's.

*"I can do nothing on My own initiative... As I hear, I judge; and My judgment is just because I do not seek My own will, but the will of Him who sent Me."* (John 5:30)

No believer can possess Christ's thinking and at the same time be arrogant. In Paul's epistle, we also read,

*Have this attitude* [humility] *in yourselves which was also in Christ Jesus.* (Philippians 2:5)

In other words, we must let Bible doctrine, which is the thinking of Christ, be the lens through which we examine and live our lives. No believer can be saturated with sound Bible doctrine, apply it correctly and consistently, and still be arrogant. *The KJV Rainbow Study Bible* summarizes this concept beautifully: "What goes into our minds comes out as our actions...We have no basis for pride except in our perfect example, Jesus Christ."

Certainly, the apostle Paul had developed a mental attitude of humility when he wrote in Philippians,

*Do nothing from selfishness or empty conceit, but with humility of mind, let each of you regard one another as more important than himself.* (Philippians 2:3)

A compelling question is: Do you regard others as more important than yourself?

Likewise, Paul challenged the Colossians:

*And so, as those who have been chosen of God, holy and beloved, put on a heart of compassion, <u>humility</u>, gentleness and patience, bearing with one another, and forgiving each other. Whoever has a complaint against anyone, just as the Lord forgave you, so also should you.* (Colossians 3:12-13)

As we previously established, Paul could not have warned or admonished the Philippians and Colossians if he had not carefully considered the basis for his warnings, the teaching of Jesus Christ directly to him. Conversely, if he hadn't diligently considered those words before penning them under the ministry of the Holy Spirit, he would have been the most pious, egocentric, self-centered, self-deceptive, and unapprised hypocrite in all of Scripture. But he wasn't because He imitated Christ. He said to the Corinthians,

*Be imitators of me just as <u>I also am of Christ</u>.* (I Corinthians 11:1)

By this we know that Paul carefully considered every word he spoke or wrote. He was neither bragging nor arrogant when he challenged the Corinthians. Without question, Paul's humility erected a fortress of grace-thinking in his soul. In fact, in eternity, we will have the privilege of witnessing the Lord's decoration of the greatest apostle in Christendom.

Now, we are ready to tap into the mind of a man whose grace-orientation continues to echo in the halls of Christian history.

## GRACE-ORIENTATION

Grace-orientation and humility are two sides of the same coin. We cannot attain a state of humility in the spiritual arena without being grace-oriented. Let me repeat:

*But He gives greater [super] grace. Therefore, it says, God is opposed to the proud [the arrogant believer], but gives grace to the humble.* (James 4:6)

Without question, Paul's salvation experience was the foundation of his grace-orientation. Here was an unbeliever committed to destroying Christianity and those who bore its name. He tortured and imprisoned Christians wherever he found them. On the road to Damascus, armed with high-powered rage against the Church, perhaps poised to inflict the greatest injury ever to Christianity, he met the Lord and was converted to Christianity by faith alone in Christ alone. Paul knew he was the greatest crusader against Christ—that had been his life's goal, and so he could barely believe that he was still breathing after he heard the Lord's voice reciting the indictment against him. He had been Christ's avowed enemy!

May I ask you, in light of what Paul did to Christians, did he deserve to be saved? Of course not! Let me direct this question more pointedly: Think of how you were before the Lord found you. Did you deserve to be saved? An emphatic NO to that, too. Was your life any better than Paul's? You'd better believe not! You were just as worthless, helpless, hopeless, and depraved as he was. We all are. Your answers to these questions are vital to measuring your understanding of grace.

In a review of his life before God graced him out, Paul lamented,

*It is a trustworthy* [Greek: πιστοφ, *pistos* = worthy to be believed] *statement, deserving full acceptance, that Christ Jesus came into the world to save sinners, among whom I am foremost of all.* (I Timothy 1:15)

Yes, you read it correctly! Paul accurately described himself as the worst sinner in human history! Because God the Holy Spirit guided Paul as he wrote these words, we know them to be true.

Not surprisingly, the word *grace* occurs 170 times in the Bible, and the greatest apostle in human history, Paul, used it more than ninety three times in his epistles.

I have no doubt that no one in all of Scripture, with the exception of Christ in His humanity and possibly Moses, had a greater grip on grace than the apostle Paul! He couldn't finish an epistle without an outpouring of his understanding of the grace of his God. Grace, to Paul, was the air he breathed in and the air he breathed out. He was a trophy of grace!

## EXAMPLES OF THE CORRECT APPLICATION OF DOCTRINE

The truth of grace must soak into our souls and leak out in our thinking and actions. No serious student of the Word of God doubts that the application of Bible doctrine is the most difficult spiritual undertaking in a believer's life. We can't possibly apply the doctrines we've learned under our own puny, worthless power. Only through the empowerment ministry of God the Holy Spirit, who works within us when we have no unconfessed sin in our lives, can we glorify God through our actions, words, and thoughts. With this in mind, I'll throw out a random sampling of the correct application of biblical principles.

- *Passing the Power Lust Temptation*: Through application of the Bible doctrine resident in a believer's soul, he never seeks to be promoted in any way. He insulates himself against such temptations with the shimmering truth that true promotion comes only from the Lord. Further, he knows that his happiness in this life has no connection to promotion or the praise from others. He is content in all circumstances—happy when promoted—equally happy when demoted!
- *Passing the Temptation to Control Others:* The mature believer outright rejects the temptation to make "one-mold-fit-all." He reminds himself that God has given each individual the ability to make his own decisions and to operate within the limits that God allows him. Thus, he restrains himself from interfering with God's decree of freedom of choice. He allows others the freedom to succeed or fail—without letting himself judge either.
- *Passing the Temptation to Seek the Praise from Others*: Suppose a doctrinal believer contributes a large amount of money to a local church or missionary organization. Armed with the Bible doctrine in his soul, he rejects the lust to have his gift recognized. He doesn't want the pastor to publicize his name. He neither seeks applause nor a letter of praise from the congregation. Rather, the doctrine in his soul causes him to rejoice at his ability to give back a small token of all God has given him, recognizing the great honor and privilege accorded him by God in allowing him to participate in His service.
- *Passing the Temptation of 'Bragamony':* Suppose a believer is tempted to give a 'bragamony' about all he is doing for the Lord. Using the doctrine in his soul, he refuses to make his service an issue. Instead, with joy, he embraces all that God is able to do for and through him because of His Son, Jesus Christ. He recognizes that both his salvation and his call to be a co-laborer with God are evidence of the grace of God. He rejects any attempt to bring glory to himself, instead giving the glory to God, the Provider of everything.
- *Passing the Temptation to Grab God's Glory*: Suppose a believer takes an inventory of his successes and is tempted to credit them to his own hard work and persistence. Instead, through the doctrine in his soul, he slams the brakes on such temptation. Inside his soul, he identifies with Paul's words after his own inventory: "But by the *grace* of God I am what I am." (I Corinthians 15:10)

# CHAPTER SEVEN
## THE BUILDING BLOCKS OF PAUL'S GRACE-ORIENTATION

Already in our study, we have examined Paul's salvation experience during his encounter with the Lord on his way to Damascus. This event became a landmark of grace in his soul. The phenomenal truth of his salvation is seen in Ephesians 2:1,

*And you were dead in your trespasses and sins.* (Ephesians 2:1)

*Dead* is the key word that sheds light on grace. This adjective in the Greek is νεκροω, *nekros*. *The Lexical Aids to the New Testament* (a Greek dictionary) explains spiritual death this way: "Having one's soul separated from the enlivening influences of the divine light and spirit as a dead body is from those of the material light and air, and consequently having no hope of life eternal."

Before we proceed, we need to ask an essential question to help us tap into the reservoir of Paul's grace thinking. To answer the question, we may need pencils and blank sheets of paper. On the blank page, list nine things a dead person is capable of doing. Well...let's make it easier. List just one thing. Crazy question, isn't it? Is your paper still blank?

Yet many teach that a spiritually dead person must make Christ Lord of his life to be saved or must invite Christ into his heart. Foolishness! False teachers actually peddle these notions of nonsense!

We are just as helpless in spiritual death as in physical death in that we can do nothing to cause our own salvation. Water baptism can't give spiritual life and a human spirit to our spiritually dead soul any more than sprinkling a corpse with water can give it physical life. Neither can any of the other idiotic ideas that false teachers have added to faith alone in Christ alone for salvation!

A dead person is totally and completely incapable of doing a thing for himself. A cadaver is always at the mercy of the living. Were it not for the law, those living could just let dead bodies rot away on the surface of the earth! The dead have no say in the matter! In the same way, the spiritually dead, which means all of mankind before salvation, are at the mercy of the living God who could have chosen to let us rot in our spiritually dead state. Because we're spiritually dead, we have no say! But God in his mercy elected to work out a solution for man's salvation. Paul said it best in Ephesians 2:4:

*God, being rich in mercy because of His great love with which He loved us, even when we were dead in our transgressions, made us alive together with Christ (by grace you have been saved) and raised*

*us up with Him, and seated us with Him in the heavenly places, in Christ Jesus.* (Ephesians 2:4-6)

In Scripture, mercy is synonymous with compassion and pity. The Greek word for mercy, ελεοφ, *eleos,* means to have special and immediate regard to the misery that is the consequence of sin. As an unbeliever, Paul was helpless and hopeless when he experienced God's compassion and pity. We can say that God's love begat mercy, and mercy begat an act of grace.

The Greek word for *saved* is σοζο, *sozo,* which in the perfect tense means saved at one point in time so that salvation is perpetuated for all eternity. Gracious God makes our eternal salvation permanent.

As we now dissect Ephesians 2:5-6, don't let your mind wander. Pay close attention because we are looking intently into the networking of Paul's grace-thinking. First, let's handle the five phrases in these two verses.

1. *When we were dead in our transgressions:* We have already established that the word *dead* indicates total helplessness. To further our point, picture a huge chasm. On one side stands helpless, sinful man; on the other side stands righteous, perfect God. What can man, a spiritually dead person before salvation, do to cross this great gulf to get to the Father? Walk an aisle? Be baptized? Dedicate his life to the Lord? Do good works? Do penance? No! No! No! Dead men can do absolutely nothing to gain salvation! Only God's grace can bridge the gap between dead mankind and Himself. The necessary grace is found in the Cross of Christ.

   *God demonstrates His own* [unfailing] *love toward us in that while we were yet sinners* [spiritually dead], *Christ died* [as a substitute] *for us.* (Romans 5:8)

   Paul's comprehension of this truth cemented his soul's Super Structure of grace-orientation.

2. *Made us alive together with Christ:* Who makes us alive? God or helpless man? God, of course! By means of the baptism of the Holy Spirit (I Corinthians 12:13), everyone who believes in Christ alone is entered into union with Him, a state which theologians refer to as positional sanctification or positional holiness. Make no mistake about it; God alone did the work of salvation. We have no room to boast about our salvation when we come face-to-face with this Biblical truth:

   *But by His* [God's] *doing* [minus your assistance] *you are in* [union with] *Christ Jesus, who became to us... righteousness and sanct-*

*ification and redemption, so that, just as it is written, "LET HIM WHO BOASTS, BOAST IN THE LORD."* (I Corinthians 1:30-31) Salvation is the quintessence and beauty of unearned grace. It is grace in action, doing for us what we cannot do for ourselves.

3. *By grace you have been saved*: Though we've said it before, let's be emphatic and say it again: Man's salvation has nothing to do with his efforts—good or bad! Works of any kind have no bearing on salvation. As stated in Isaiah 64:6, "...all our righteous deeds are like filthy rags [menstrual cloths]." For those who still think they can, through their works, bridge the gap that separates them from God, listen once again to Paul.

*For if Abraham was justified by works, he has something to boast about; but not before God* [because he wasn't justified by works]. *For what does the Scripture say? And <u>Abraham believed God</u>* [faith plus nothing], *and it* [his faith alone in Christ alone] *was reckoned to him as righteousness. Now to the one who works, his wage is not reckoned a favor* [or grace], *but as what is due. But to the one who does not work but believes in Him who justifies the ungodly* [every sinner, and therefore, all mankind], *his faith is credited as righteousness.* (Romans 4:2-5)

Paul rests his defense of salvation by faith alone in Christ alone with the doctrine of "grace and works cannot be mixed."

*But if it* [salvation] *is by grace, it is no longer on the basis of works, otherwise grace is no longer grace.* (Romans 11:6)

I am baffled by the salvation-by-works crowd who say they believe in grace, "BUT..." they always add. I say...but what? Our salvation is either by grace or by works; that's exactly what the above verse underscores! It cannot be both! It cannot be mixed! The word *but* does not follow grace—ever. Grace must be allowed to stand-alone! No such thing as "grace but" or "grace plus" can be found anywhere in the entire Bible.

Consider Paul's reaction to the Galatians, who, having entered the spiritual race by means of grace—faith alone in Christ alone (Galatians 1:6) now wanted to augment the grace of salvation with works. (Galatians 3:3) In reacting to this arrogant error, Paul thundered:

*You foolish Galatians, who has bewitched you* [!]? *... This is the only thing I want to find out from you: Did you receive the Spirit* [the Holy Spirit] *by works... or by hearing with faith? Are you so foolish? Having begun by the Spirit* [through faith alone in Christ alone], *are you now being perfected by the flesh* [your own works]*?* (Galatians 3:1-3)

Paul's question, "Who has bewitched you?" is directed to anyone who thinks that his formula for salvation is better than God's grace formula. Paul wasn't alone in his stand on grace. Luke recorded Peter's words in Acts,

*And God, who knows the heart, bore witness to them* [Gentiles], *giving them the Holy Spirit, just as He also did to us* [Jews]*; and He made no distinction between us and them, cleansing their hearts* [because of faith in Christ]. *Now, therefore, why do you put God to the test* [why are you picking a fight against God] *by placing upon the neck of the disciples* [believers] *a yoke* [i.e. legalism, works], *which neither our fathers nor we have been able to bear?* <u>*But we believed that we are saved through the grace of the Lord Jesus,*</u> *in the same way as they also were.* (Acts 15:8-11)

You see, Peter conceded that no one in the past was successful in bearing the yoke of salvation by works, nor can anyone in the present be successful! So, if you are a believer who is making another believer's life miserable by yoking him with works and legalism for salvation, yoke him no more! You need to cease and desist in a hurry from torturing other believers who bear the mark of grace because of who and what God is. Stop telling them they must add anything to faith alone in Christ alone to be saved. Stop placing your arrogant false teaching above God's grace.

*Raised us up with Him:* The issue of *raising you up* takes us back to verse one. As unbelievers, we are in a spiritually dead state—unable to help ourselves or God. Can a dead person raise himself up? Emphatically no! Someone with other than a lifeless body would have to do that. God is that Someone. Paul's understanding of this Truth caused him to chill-out and be raised another notch on the Super Structure of grace-orientation. Paul could not elevate himself in the spiritual arena, nor can we. Just as surely as with Paul, when we have a hold on this subject of salvation by grace, we, too, will begin to have a mental attitude of grace and gratitude to God the Father. At that point, we will be cuddled and wrapped in the blanket of God's amazing grace.

The substitutionary death of Christ on the Cross for the entire human race gives everyone equal privilege and potential to believe in Him and be justified by God the Father. Note that we said potential. Christ's death on the Cross as a substitute for everyone does not guarantee salvation for all, a false view held by heretical teachers. For those who reject Christ, the Cross becomes the only basis for their condemnation.

*He who believes in Him is not judged. He who does not believe has been judged already because he has not believed in the name of the only begotten Son of God.* (John 3:18)

*And He* [the Holy Spirit], *when He comes, will convict the world concerning sin* [singular—the sin of unbelief]*... because they do not believe in Me* [the Lord Jesus Christ]. (John 16:8-9)

The Bible is clear: Jesus Christ bore our sins in His own body on the Cross. (I Peter 2:24) He paid the penalty for the sins of the entire human race. (I John 2:2) Paul put it this way:

*Knowing this, that our old self* [sin nature] *was crucified with Him.* (Romans 6:6)

When anyone believes in Christ as personal Savior, Christ's substitutionary spiritual death on the Cross becomes experiential, meaning no longer potential but actual. As a result, God's righteousness and eternal life are imputed to the new believer, and he is automatically entered into union with Christ where he also shares Christ's righteousness and sanctification. (I Corinthians 1:30)

That's the concept of water baptism before the canon of Scripture was completed in 96 A.D. In Romans, we are asked,

*Or do you not know that all of us who have been baptized into Christ Jesus* [positional sanctification] *have been baptized into His death? Therefore, we have been buried with Him through baptism into death in order that as Christ was raised from the dead through the glory of the Father, so we too might walk in newness of life.* (Romans 6:3-4)

When an early Church Age believer was immersed in water, he held his breath, thereby identifying himself with Christ's death. He resumed breathing when he was raised from the water, signifying his new position in glory with Christ. Thus, water baptism was a teaching aid— no more, no less. Water baptism had nothing to do with salvation.

4.  *Seated us with Him in the heavenly places in Christ Jesus*: This phrase is connected to the last one we examined. The action of seating us is totally God's. He does everything. He is the One who raised us up and the very One who seated us with Christ in heaven. At this very moment, whether you realize it or not, the real you, because you have believed in Christ for salvation, is already seated in Christ in the heavenly places! In Colossians, the Holy Spirit, through Paul, tells us,

*For you have died and your life is hidden with Christ in God.*
(Colossians 3:3)

How could your salvation be more secure? You are hidden in Christ, and Christ is hidden in God the Father!

## PRINCIPLES

- We were rotting in sin, depraved, helpless, and hopeless when, by His grace, God saved us.
- At salvation, every believer is indwelt by the members of the Godhead, shares in Christ's righteousness and sanctification, is given God's imputed righteousness, and has the enabling power of the Holy Spirit and the written Word of God at his disposal.
- After salvation, even with all the divine assets that God gives us, we still fail Him whenever we work in the energy of the flesh. Paul personified this principle and called himself *a wretched man.* (Romans 7:24)
- Our resurrection at the Rapture of the church will reveal the surpassing riches of God's grace despite our failures in time.

## SALVATION IS THE GIFT OF GOD

This brings us to verses 8 and 9 of Ephesians Chapter 2.

*For by grace you have been saved through faith; and that* [salvation] *not of yourselves, it is the gift of God; not as a result of works, so that no one should boast.* (Ephesians 2:8-9)

In these verses, Paul explicitly separated grace from works with regard to salvation. Without doing any exegesis of these two verses, we want to underline and briefly develop the phrase *it is the gift of God.*

The exchange of a gift always involves two parties. Let's use some questions to make our point. Who does the work when it comes to giving—the giver or the receiver? Is there any work in giving? Yes. What about receiving—any work? No.

I take pleasure in giving gifts to friends and relatives. But first I have to go shopping and spend ample time looking for the perfect gift. When I find one, I pay for it, take it home, and wrap it with beautiful wrapping paper. Then I present the gift to the receiver. The receiver simply receives. That's all. I do all the work from start to finish.

The same is true of all our grace gifts from God, beginning with salvation. He does all the work. We do nothing.

Generally, we give gifts to people because we know them or have rapport with them. If we think of God's gift in this manner, we become guilty of humanizing God. When it comes to the gift of salvation, the recipients are depraved, undeserving, and below the bottom rung of unworthiness. Paul first realized his unworthiness on his trip to Damascus.

No question about it: When you truly understand *The Biblical Doctrine of Salvation,*[6] the erection of a Super Structure of grace-orientation in your soul becomes inevitable! And, when you understand the doctrine of hamartiology (sin), you recognize your status as abysmally unworthy.

## THE ETERNAL SECURITY OF THE BELIEVER

Eternal security means that once we are saved through faith alone in Christ alone nothing we do or others do to us can take that salvation from us. Christ did all the work in saving us. His work is perfect. Since our salvation rests on Christ and not ourselves, we can be assured we will never lose it.

Clearly, a believer who rejects the doctrine of *The Eternal Security of the Believer.*[7] cannot become grace-oriented. Paul understood this subject more than anyone in the Bible with the exception of Christ in His human nature. In Romans, Paul proclaimed,

> *For I am convinced* [both from revelation directly from Jesus Christ and from study of Scripture] *that neither death, nor life, nor angels* [elect and fallen], *nor principalities, nor things present, nor things to come* [the Rapture and eternity], *nor powers* [including God's who cannot undermine His own work], *nor height, nor depth, nor any other created being, shall be able to separate us* [those in union with Christ] *from the love of God, which is* [rooted] *in Christ Jesus.* (Romans 8:38-39)

The idea of eternal security is a mouthful of sour milk to legalistic believers. Many object to this Truth because they believe people will lose their desire to serve God if the potential for loss of salvation can't be dangled over their heads. Such an argument doesn't hold water with anyone who knows the value of positional sanctification,[8] our permanent position in union with Christ gained at salvation. When we understand that our salvation from start to finish has nothing whatsoever to do with us, we will be aglow with grace-orientation—a Christian at ease!

## GOD'S GRACE ATTITUDE TOWARD PAUL

> …And from everyone [every Church Age believer] who has been given much, much will be required. (Luke 12:48b)

---

[6] Book by Rev. Moses C. Onwubiko
[7] Booklet by Rev. Moses C. Onwubiko
[8] *Biblical Doctrine of Salvation*, pp. 56-62.

The *much* that is required is our fulfillment of God's plan for our lives through the utilization of the filling of the Holy Spirit and knowledge of the Word of God. Paul was acutely aware that God had done everything for him and that he hadn't earned it or done anything to deserve it. God's grace was not limited just to his salvation and eternal security but included his deliverance from daily dangers (II Timothy 3:11), his provision, and successes as well as his rewards in time and eternity (II Timothy 4:7-8). In just such a way, God graces us out if we trust Him and follow His plan for our lives.

Paul was awed by God's grace. No wonder he unequivocally came to the conclusion,

*But by the grace of God I am what I am...* (I Corinthians 15:10a)

Paul knew without doubt that he was nothing and, therefore, any successes, rewards, praise, and sustenance were directly from God, grace gifts all the way.

## SIN

Now let's talk about failures in time. The first man Adam brought sin into the world because of one negative decision (Romans 5:12), but that sin, which all mankind receives at birth, is wiped from our souls when we believe in Christ as our personal Savior. God promises to never again remember this imputed sin from Adam. (Hebrews 8:12; Romans 4:7-8) However, our post-salvation failures are by our own choice, not Adam's! We want to sin, and we choose to do it. The good news is that our post-salvation sins have no bearing on our eternal destiny; however, they can shorten our lives and deprive us of a multitude of rewards both in time and in eternity.[9]

In one of my missionary endeavors in Africa, I met a minister who told me point blank that since he had become a believer (1982), he had never committed any sin. "Woo!" was my response to him. But after I took him through the Scriptures, he changed his tune. He said, "Well, I may have made some mistakes since I became a believer." He gave sin a new name—Mistake!

The question remains, how many times have you failed God in thought or action? Or failed to trust Him? How many times did you promise God to make Bible doctrine the number one priority in your life but failed to live up to that promise? How many times have you maligned, gossiped, and judged others? Millions of times? We all fail often. No exceptions! And yet Paul affirmed,

---

[9] Onwubiko, Moses, *Biblical Doctrine of Salvation*, (pp. 56-62).

*With a shout, with the voice of the archangel and with the trumpet of God, and the dead in Christ* [loser and winner believers] *will rise first... to meet the Lord in the air.* (I Thessalonians 4:16-17)

You read it correctly! Despite our many sins, we will still be like Christ in eternity! Let's repeat that. We will have the same resurrection body as Christ!

## EXAMPLES OF THE CORRECT APPLICATION OF DOCTRINE

- When the believer meditates on his salvation, he recognizes that he was totally lost, depraved, and unable to save himself and that God in His matchless grace saved him from eternal doom.
- When the believer is tempted to add work to his salvation, he rejects the temptation and accepts Truth drawn from the inventory of Bible doctrine in his soul. For instance,

    *He* [God] *who has saved us... not according to our works, but according to His purpose and grace...* (II Timothy 1:9)

- When the fear of losing his salvation rages in a believer's soul, he calms himself by thinking the doctrines he has learned. He reminds himself that he is now God's child and, thus, cannot be unborn. He relaxes in his soul, knowing that his salvation is a gift (Ephesians 2:8-9; Romans 6:23b), which God cannot revoke. (Romans 11:29)
- When the believer is tempted to live in sin because he knows he can't lose his salvation, he pauses to remember that God administers divine discipline to His children. (Hebrews 12:6) So, instead, he pursues sound Bible doctrine with all alacrity, aiming to grow in grace, reach the high ground of spiritual maturity, and, thus, glorify God to the maximum.
- When a believer is maligned, judged, ridiculed, hated, and treated unjustly, he does not respond in kind. Rather, with the assistance of God the Holy Spirit, he remains self-composed. He shows compassion and mercy to the one who hates him. He recognizes that God has graced him out in everything. He is eager to lift the individual up to the throne of grace—praying that God will open his eyes so that he can also come to know God's grace! Of course, our spiritual growth is directly proportional to our grace-orientation toward others! The more we learn of God's grace-treatment toward us, the more eager we are to extend grace to those around us.

## ULTIMATE GRACE RESERVED

In Ephesians 2:7, we read:

*In order that in the ages to come He* [God] *might show the surpassing riches of His grace in kindness toward us in Christ Jesus.*

This verse is the nucleus, the very core, of God's grace! We could say, "You ain't seen nothing yet!" Ironically, even the apostle Paul didn't see the magnitude of what I term Ultimate Grace Reserved. Certainly, no living believer in the Lord Jesus Christ has experienced this grace. God reserves it until the death of a believer or the Rapture, "the exit resurrection." We can experience grace-upon-grace only when we are

*...absent from the body and home* [face-to-face] *with the Lord.*
(II Corinthians 5:8b)

At the Rapture, *all* believers—moral, amoral, immoral, losers and winners—will be the objects of Ultimate Grace Reserved. All believers will receive resurrection bodies, the first installment of Ultimate Grace Reserved. (I Corinthians 15:50-56)

The next installment will be given in the millennial reign of Christ when only those who glorified God through the filling of the Holy Spirit and the Bible doctrine in their souls while on earth will receive honors, decorations, and the privilege of ruling with Christ.

The next installment comes in the eternal state following the Millennium when every believer will realize the privilege of living with God forever and ever. What magnificent grace to anticipate!

*Even when we were dead in our transgressions, He* [God the Father] *made us alive together with Christ (by grace you have been saved), and raised us up with Him, and seated us with Him in the heavenly places in Christ Jesus.* (Ephesians 2:5-6)

Three actions, all of which are the handiwork of God, occur in these two verses, which we discussed in detail earlier in this book:
- God caused the believer to be alive.
- God raised the believer in the Lord from his spiritual death.
- God seated the believer with Christ in heaven.

The fourth action, the subject of verse 7, is future and is guaranteed.

*In order that in the ages to come He* [God] *might show the surpassing* [above and beyond] *riches of His grace.* (Ephesians 2:7)

In this verse, the phrase *in order that* introduces a purpose clause that results from the completed action of verses 5 and 6. If we have followed God's command to learn and apply His Word, we will receive the final installment of Ultimate Grace Reserved when God will show us more grace than our feeble minds could ever imagine, riches beyond belief, all of them eternal. Remember that these final grace gifts will be given only to those believers whose thoughts while on earth glorified God because they were His viewpoint taken directly from His Word.

Without doubt, Bible doctrine is the only compass for our spiritual journey, and undeniably, its application is the beam of light on our path. We can state this principle another way: The test of God's Word is in its application. God assures us that His Word always works. We have already delineated that the apostle Paul had an iron grip on the doctrine of grace. His soul soaked up grace like a dry sponge dropped in water, then overflowed to everyone who came in contact with him.

## PAUL'S GRACE-INSULATED MENTAL ATTITUDE

The Scripture concretely states that man is the product of his thinking. King Solomon put it this way:

*For as he thinks within himself so he is.* (Proverbs 23:7)

The first notch on the grace-orientation belt is the total realization that apart from God's grace, man is merely a heap of rubbish. This sobering truth was crystal clear to King David when he asked,

*What is man* [a heap of stinking rubble] *that You are mindful of him, the son of man that You care for him?* (Psalm 8:4).

The apostle Paul had the same thoughts when he took inventory of his life's achievements and reached this grace-thinking conclusion: *"...I am a nobody."* (II Corinthians 12:11c) With regard to his divine appointment, he said, *"I am... not fit to be called an apostle."* (I Corinthians 15:9) This statement is not a denial of his achievements; his secular and spiritual achievements were beyond that of all other men. (I Corinthians 15:10) Instead, his thinking was woven throughout with grace rather than his own merits. Thus he could say, *"But by the grace of God I am what I am."* (I Corinthians 15:10a).

How in the world can any believer, regardless of his spiritual status and achievements, ever conceive in his soul that he is what he is because of anything other than the grace of God? Indeed, grace-orientation housed Paul's thinking and kept him from becoming arrogant. That's not all! Others became beneficiaries of his wellspring of grace. We are doing so right now as we learn God's Word as taught by His servant Paul.

## GRACE-ORIENTATION TOWARD OTHERS

Ironically, the people closest to us are a major testing ground for grace-orientation. Our parents, spouse, children, mother- and father-in-laws, family members, and friends, believers as well as unbelievers, are all obnoxious people, just like us! Those we love the most have the capacity to test us the most severely. We run into them daily, and our attitude places us either with those who are honoring God or those who are failing in their spiritual journey. The Scriptures tell us that

*Love does no wrong to a neighbor* [anyone in the world]*; love, therefore, is the fulfillment of the law.* (Romans 13:10)

In other words, grace-orientation! We cannot be grace-oriented and have the slightest thought to harm a neighbor or treat our enemy as he treats us. (Romans 12:19)

Paul's grace-orientation toward other people was a perfect example of a winner believer in the spiritual battle. Let me underscore these words: Grace-orientation is not an overnight experience. It takes time to develop. Sadly, only a handful of believers ever become grace-oriented even though grace-orientation is the core of the spiritual life and the other side of virtuous love. Grace-orientation and virtue love go hand-in-hand. We cannot possess one and lack the other. That would be impossible!

The Pauline epistles bear witness to Paul's grace-attitude toward others. We have previously documented that Paul could not have said to his fellow believers, "Be imitators of me," if he weren't mindful of his spiritual life. As we've noted, Paul wasn't being arrogant when he made this statement. With that in mind, let's concentrate on two aspects of Paul's grace-orientation: His thoughtfulness of others and his generosity.

## PAUL'S THOUGHTFULNESS OF OTHERS: A COMPONENT OF HIS GRACE-ORIENTATION

Grace-orientation precludes any form of self-promotion or arrogant thinking and considers others with high esteem [Greek: *hegeomia*]. Paul fulfilled this concept with everyone, believers and unbelievers alike. Keep in mind, this doctrine doesn't mean that those with a degree in medicine or engineering should belittle themselves around someone with only a high school diploma. Instead, they must consider their attainment grace-made, grace-provided. Any education, honors, beauty, or wealth should never cause us to look down on those who have not attained our same level. Paul put it beautifully:

*For who regards you as superior? And what do you have that you did not receive [from God]?* (I Corinthians 4:7a)

Everything that you and I have passes through the pipeline of God's grace. It's that simple.

## PAUL'S GENEROSITY:
## A COMPONENT OF HIS GRACE-ORIENTATION

*Do not merely look out for your own personal interest, but also for the interests of others.* (Philippians 2:4)

This statement of grace ricochets from Paul's soul to ours as Church Age believers. Paul was a man of great compassion. Luke recorded him saying,

*You yourselves know that these hands* [of mine] *ministered to my own needs and to the men who were with me. In everything I showed you that by working hard in this manner you must help the weak* [the needy] *and remember the words of the Lord Jesus, that He Himself said, "It is more blessed to give than to receive."* (Acts 20:34-35)

That's what Paul did! He financially assisted his needy partners! As a tentmaker, he used his trade to make money whenever an opportunity presented itself. His grace-orientation compelled him to care for others who were in need. He didn't look the other way.

The apostle John put it this way,

*But whoever has the world's goods and beholds his brother in need and closes his heart against him, how does the love of God abide in him? Little children, let us not love with word or with tongue, but in deed and truth. We shall know by this that we are of the truth and shall assure our heart before Him... If our heart does not condemn us, we have confidence before God* [when we approach His throne in prayer], *and whatever we ask, we receive from Him.* (I John 3:17-22a)

Indeed, a believer's negative attitude toward the less fortunate can have an adverse effect on his prayer. King Solomon wrote,

*He who shuts his ear to the cry of the poor will cry himself and not be answered.* (Proverbs 21:13)

In James, we read,

*If a brother or sister is without clothing and in need of daily food, and one of you says to them, "Go in peace, be warmed, and be filled," and yet do not give them what is necessary* [according to your means] *for their body, what use is that?* [What kind of grace-orientation is that?] (James 2:15-16)

We could rephrase that as immature believers do, "Sister, I will lift you up before the Heavenly throne—and be sure everyone sees me doing it, but I sure won't give you anything! I've worked for all I have. Go out and do so, too!"

The great eighteenth century missionary, George Muller, once interrupted one of his prayer meetings, which was focusing on a particular need, by taking a piece of paper and writing, "George will give 50 pounds.".[10]. He passed the paper around so that others could pledge as they purposed in their souls. After the paper had circulated, he said, "Brethren, now we can pray in good conscience." What a marvelous application of the doctrinal truth in James!

The well being of other believers becomes a joyful responsibility for a grace-oriented believer with Bible doctrine stored in his soul. Indeed, the believer who has the spiritual gift of generosity constantly finds himself on the giving end. However, caring or giving in itself does not make one grace-oriented. Grace-orientation springs from spiritual growth. To be sure, Paul was a mature believer, and, consequently, the elect angels beheld with gladness his life, a life of giving, lived to God's glory.

---

[10] A pound is a unit of British currency.

# CHAPTER NINE
## GRACE-ORIENTATION IN THE LIFE OF JOSHUA

We consider it wise to pause, review our previous studies, meditate, ask questions that are pertinent to our spiritual lives, and examine the lives of an Old Testament winner believer who applied the doctrine in his soul for God's glory. So far, we have briefly covered the historical background of the great apostle Paul. With the exception of the humanity of Christ, who was also called Apostle, Paul was the greatest apostle of all time.

We have also examined in detail Saul's enthusiastic desire to serve God before his conversion, how in his zeal he became a nightmare to believers in the Lord Jesus Christ by torturing, imprisoning, and aiding in their martyrdom. In the process, we noted the principle that *a right thing done in a wrong way is wrong.* Paul's intention to serve God before he was converted into Christianity is a perfect example of this timeless principle.

Saul (a.k.a. Paul) was, for sure, an enduring nightmare for early Christians. Was Saul a likely candidate for God's pure grace? Could he possibly spend all of eternity in the presence of the King of kings? The answer is a resounding YES! Saul was intercepted by grace on his way to Damascus. We saw God's grace gift to him, namely, the imputation of God's righteousness and eternal life, imputations available solely through faith alone in Christ alone.

Above all, we saw God's grace in action in commissioning Paul, a man who accurately called himself the worst sinner in human history. (I Timothy 1:15) This conversion experience and commission became the foundation of a grace Super Structure in his soul.

In addition, we looked at Paul's post-salvation lifestyle—how his soul was awash in the ocean of God's Word, banked by divine viewpoint and a grace mental attitude. Indeed, a brief summary doesn't do justice to all that grace did for Paul and will do for those who persevere in God's Word.

Has grace hit you between the eyes and taken hold of every facet of your soul? Or are you a legalistic believer? While self-righteous believers denigrate another church member or even the pastor, do you "hold the cloaks" as Paul did at the fatal stoning of Stephen?

Legalism often goes hand-in-hand with arrogance. The Scripture commands,

> *Test yourselves to see if you are in the faith* [your lifestyle is aligned with sound doctrine and application]. *Examine yourselves... "* (II Corinthians 13:5)

You should take a minute or so every day to inventory your soul. You may wish to start by asking yourself these vital questions: Since I became a believer in the Lord Jesus Christ and became acquainted with expository

Bible teaching or with Grace Evangelistic Ministries or any other ministry that is doctrinally sound, have I made any spiritual progress? (II Peter 3:18) Am I advancing to the high ground of spiritual maturity? Do my daily conversations and actions testify that I am, indeed, a believer who is heavenly-minded? (Colossians 3:1-2) Can I concur with the apostle Paul when he declared,

> But whatever things were gain to me, those things I have counted as loss for the sake of Christ. More than that, I count all things but loss in view of the surpassing value of knowing Christ Jesus my Lord, for whom I have suffered the loss of all things, and count them but rubbish in order that I may gain Christ. (Philippians 3:7-8)

As an open letter *"known and read by all men"* does your lifestyle draw unbelievers to Christ and believers to the sound Bible doctrine you love to learn? (II Corinthians 3:3) Sure, you may be taking in Bible doctrine on a daily basis, but the question remains, does the doctrine you learn every day affect your mental attitude toward God, self, and others? Do you have good and true rapport with your Heavenly Father and people in general? (Luke 2:52) Like the apostle Paul, is your spiritual life a trophy of grace? How do you deal with those who don't seem to have the same viewpoint? How do you handle the problems that confront you daily? Do you keep on drinking from the spring of happiness even in the midst of chaos? When you stand at the Rugged Gate of Physical Death with just a few days or seconds before departure from this earth, will you confidently, humbly, and graciously make Paul's words you own?

> I have fought the good fight; I have finished the course; I have kept the faith [I have applied Bible doctrine to God's glory]; in the future there is laid up for me the crown of righteousness, which the Lord, the righteous Judge, will award to me on that day; and not only to me, but also to all [who will fulfill the grace plan of God] who love His appearing. (II Timothy 4:7-8)

The answers to these questions are a private matter between you and the Lord. As we've learned, the truth of the matter is that our spiritual lives are not measured by the amount of Bible doctrine we know but by the amount of doctrine we apply on a regular basis.

Let me dogmatically say it again: Our spiritual lives and glorification of God in this fallen world are not measured by the amount of systematic theology and Bible doctrine we know, but by the amount we know and apply. In the end, oceans of happiness do not belong to the believer with an arsenal of doctrine in his soul but to those who routinely make application from that arsenal of Truth to life's exigencies.

Christ often gave emphasis to this phenomenal concept. (e.g. Luke 11:28) The Messiah, Truth personified, stated that,

> *Blessed* [happy] *is he who heeds* [pays close attention through perception and application] *the words of the prophesy of this book.* (Revelation 22:7b)

## JOSHUA: A BELIEVER WHO APPLIED GOD'S WORD

We know that God uses and blesses prepared believers who have, through perception and application of Bible doctrine, become grace-oriented. These believers possess spiritual integrity and the capacity to appreciate and enjoy God's immeasurable blessings. They also know that God does not, cannot, and will not bless them because of who and what they are or because of anything they accomplish in the energy of the flesh. More exactly, He blesses them based on their capacity to appreciate His grace. The good news is that this capacity can be developed through the utilization of simple grace assets, namely, perception of Bible doctrine and its application under the mentorship of the Holy Spirit. We will now study Joshua's successful application of biblical Truth to his life.

Joshua, the Ephraimite, was born in Egyptian bondage around 1500 B.C. We believe that while in slavery in Egypt, his father, Nun, introduced Joshua to the God of Abraham, Isaac, and Jacob. Prior to Israel's liberation from Egyptian slavery, Joshua witnessed the omnipotent hand of God work ten miracles. These miracles became the foundation for his faith-rest life, his divine viewpoint, and his application of God's Word. After God miraculously liberated the Jews from Egypt, Joshua became a diligent student in Moses' expository Bible class. He advanced rapidly in spiritual growth and developed confidence in God's Word. Above all, he witnessed God's faithfulness throughout their journey in the wilderness, both in guidance and daily provision.

The question for you is this: Has the Lord been as faithful to you as He was to Joshua both in provision and guidance? Absolutely! Has He been gracious to you in every way? He has been because He is God.

PRINCIPLE: It's not all about you; it's all about God. We are here in a fallen world for one reason only: Maximum glorification of God! Any other reason is foolishness and at best satanic.

Prior to Joshua's appointment and promotion by God to leader of the Jews, God tested him on his viewpoint. Would he use God's viewpoint under severe testing? In 1445 B.C., Joshua, representing Ephraim, one of the twelve tribes, was sent to spy on Canaan in the Promised Land. (Numbers

13) When the men representing the twelve tribes came back from spying, all except Joshua and Caleb reported,

*"We went in to the land where you sent us; and it certainly does flow with milk and honey* [just as the Lord promised in Exodus 3:7-8] *and this is its fruit* [as evidence]. *Nevertheless, the people who live in the land are strong* [giants!], *and the cities are fortified and very large... We are not able to go up against the people, for they are too strong for us* [human viewpoint]. *"* (Numbers 13:27, 29-31)

Through human viewpoint, these men saw unconquerable giants and impassable fortresses! They panicked.

As a believer in the Lord Jesus Christ, when you look at your problems what do you see? An impassable wall? A hopeless situation? Do "giants" blind you to God's solution as found in His Word?

These faithless Jewish spies did not exaggerate their findings. In fact, modern archeologists have found numerous large walled fortresses throughout Palestine. Some were as large as ten acres, making invasion by foreign armies extremely difficult.[11]

Because of the frightened spies' majority report, the entire congregation of Israel (with the exception of Moses, Joshua, and Caleb) had panic attacks. Their blood ran ice-cold! Sadly, they completely blotted God's miracles out from their frame of reference. They instantly switched from God's viewpoint to man's viewpoint. Finally, an angry God confronted Moses.

*The Lord said to Moses, 'How long will this people spurn* [Hebrew: *na'ats* = scorn with the idea of disdain for one who formerly received favorable attention] *Me? And how long will they not believe in Me, despite all the signs which I performed in their midst?* [How long will it be before these believers begin to apply doctrine?] (Numbers 14:11)

God directed this question to the Jews in the wilderness more than 3,000 years ago, expecting believers in the Church Age to redirect it toward themselves. It's imperative that you ask yourself the same question that I ask myself every day, which is: Am I applying Bible doctrine on a regular basis to God's glory? Again, remember, life isn't about you. It's all about Christ and His efficacious sacrifice on the Cross. It's all about God and His unique plan for the Church Age. It's all about our Father's glory.

Because of the divine viewpoint in their souls, Joshua and Caleb, the two spies in fellowship with God, ignored the frightened bleating of their

---

[11] Zodhiates, Spiro (NASB, 1995 footnote), 201.

fellow spies, applied doctrine from their souls, and reached the divinely acceptable conclusion,

*"We should by all means go up and take possession of it* [the Promised Land], *for we shall surely overcome it."* (Numbers 13:30)

While the rest of the Jews had their eyes on the problem—giants and seemingly impenetrable fortresses, Joshua, through the lens of God's divine viewpoint acquired from the Bible doctrine he had previously stored in his soul, had his eyes on the divine solution, absolutely confident that God keeps His promises (Exodus 3:7,8; Hebrews 10:23) and with a firm understanding that, as Jesus Christ declared while on earth,

*Heaven and earth shall pass away, but My* [God's] *Words will not pass away.* (Matthew 24:35)

Because of Joshua's firm faith in God and his dogmatic expression of that faith, the entire congregation sought to stone him, but God intervened (Numbers 14:10) because He had special plans for His faithful servant, Joshua. Near the end of Moses' ministry in 1406 B.C. and prior to Moses's death, God in His matchless grace called upon Joshua, a man of proven spiritual integrity, to be Moses's successor and the Israelites' new leader. (Numbers 27:18) Along with this God-given privilege, the Lord spelled out to Joshua, just as He did for others in the Old Testament and now for you and me in the Bible, the exact way by which he could successfully complete the spiritual race. To Joshua, He instructed,

*"This book of the law* [the whole realm of Bible doctrine] *shall not depart from your mouth, but you shall keep on meditating on it day and night, so that you may be careful to do according to all that is written in it* [apply all of God's Word]*; for* [only] *then you will make your way prosperous, then you will have* [super abundant] *success."* (Joshua 1:8)

In the above verse, God delineated a simple formula for the spiritual success and blessing of not only Joshua but also of the Church Age believer.

The Filling of the Holy Spirit {**FHS**} + Perception of Basic Bible Doctrine {**PBBD**} + Application of Basic Bible Doctrine {**ABBD**} = Spiritual Momentum {**SM**}

**FHS + PBBD + ABBD = SM**

The Filling of the Holy Spirit {**FHS**} + Spiritual Momentum {**SM**} + Perception of Advanced Bible Doctrine {**PABD**} + Spiritual Testing {**ST**}

+ Application of Advanced Bible Doctrine {**AABD**} = Spiritual Focus {**SF**} + Grace-Orientation {**GO**} + Spiritual Capacity {**SC**}

**FHS + SM + PABD + ST + AABD = SF + GO + SC**

The Filling of the Holy Spirit {**FHS**} + Spiritual Capacity {**SC**} + Grace-Orientation {**GO**} + Spiritual Sense of Destiny {**SSD**} + Advanced Spiritual Testing {**AST**} = Super Abundance of Blessing in Time {**SABT**}

**FHS + SC + GO + SSD + AST = SABT**

Super Abundance of Blessing in Time {**SABT**} + Ultimate Spiritual Testing {**UST**} = Surpassing Decoration in Heaven {**SDH**} + Ultimate Reward in the Eternal State {URES}

**SABT + UST = SDH + URES**

You don't need to memorize the above formula word for word because this computation will happen naturally as you advance to the high ground of spiritual maturity. However, a good understanding of it will help accelerate your advance in the spiritual life.

Paul, in his farewell address to the Ephesians after giving them three years of face-to-face Bible expository teaching, said,

*And now I commend you to God and to* <u>*the word of His grace*</u> [accurate Bible teaching], *which is able to build you up* [give you capacity] *and to give you the inheritance* [blessings in time and eternity for mature believers] *among those who are sanctified* [believers who have fulfilled the plan of God for their lives]. (Acts 20:32)

PRINCIPLE: Our blessings in time and eternity are directly proportional to our spiritual growth and capacity to appreciate them.

# CHAPTER TEN

# SPIRITUAL WARFARE

I consider it wise to examine the filling of the Holy Spirit, the word of His grace, and doctrinal application mechanics before concluding this expositional teaching.

## THE FILLING OF THE HOLY SPIRIT

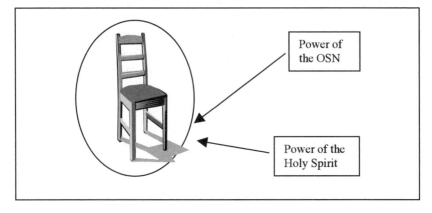

Power of the OSN

Power of the Holy Spirit

### DIAGRAM OF SPIRITUAL WARFARE

The above diagram illustrates the functions of the Holy Spirit and the Old Sin Nature in a believer's soul. The box represents the believer's body in which God the Father, Son, and Holy Spirit (I Corinthians 3:16, II Corinthians 6:16; Colossians 1:27) as well as the Old Sin Nature (OSN) reside. (Romans 7:17) The circle represents the believer's soul with a gate of entrance. The chair illustrates the command post of the soul.

Two powers operate inside the body of every believer, namely the power of the Old Sin Nature and that of the Holy Spirit. The OSN fights tooth and nail to serve Satan's purpose while the Holy Spirit endeavors to fulfill God's plan for our lives. Both are in conflict, each wanting control of the command post of our souls, the center of our actions and decisions, whether good or bad. Only one can be at the helm of the soul at a time. The apostle Paul taught this phenomenal doctrine to the Galatians by explaining,

> *But I say, walk by the Spirit* [keep on allowing the Holy Spirit to control the command post of your soul], *and you will not carry out the desire of your flesh* [the OSN]. *For* [purpose clause] *the flesh* [OSN] *sets its desire against the Spirit* [wanting to recapture the command post of the soul], *and the Spirit against the flesh; for these* [two dynamic powers] *are in opposition*

*to* [at war with] *one another, so that you may not* [volition] *do the things you please.* (Galatians 5:16-17)

## PRINCIPLES

- A believer's soul is a battleground for spiritual warfare.
- All actions, divine or carnal, are processed and carried out from the soul.
- The command post of the soul accommodates for operational purposes both the power of the OSN and that of the Holy Spirit. In other words, the Holy Spirit and the Sin Nature make frequent trips to your soul in order to fulfill God's plan or Satan's objectives respectively.
- A believer never commits a sin unless the OSN is in control of the command post of his soul.
- When God the Holy Spirit controls his soul, the believer has manifold, but potential opportunities to glorify God. Note that I said potential. Many believers erroneously think that all they need to do in their spiritual lives is take in doctrine on a daily basis and acknowledge their sins to God whenever they fail. (I John 1:9) These believers assume that because they do these two things, they are living the spiritual life. Nothing is farther from the truth. The filling of the Holy Spirit is never an end in itself but the means, the Energizer, for the execution of God's plan. A believer can be controlled (filled) by the Holy Spirit and yet fail to glorify God. He can have learned tons of Bible doctrine and be a spiritual failure. Only by applying the Truth stored in his soul under the power of the Holy Spirit does he glorify God and fulfill His plan for his life.
- Even when the Holy Spirit resides in the soul of a believer or is seated at the command post, He does not live the believer's life for him. He only provides the spiritual power necessary for the believer to accomplish *humanly impossible* tasks, such as impersonal love for all mankind. (John 14:16; Zechariah 4:6) The apostle Peter was a typical example. Prior to the indwelling and filling of the Holy Spirit, Peter proved a coward. During our Lord's trial, a slave girl approached Peter and identified him as Christ's follower, but Peter categorically and vehemently denied ever knowing Christ, and he did so with an oath! (Matthew 26:71-74) That's right—with an oath! However, on the Day of Pentecost, Peter was both indwelt and filled with the Holy Spirit (Acts 2), and so he fearlessly and boldly preached Christ and even called the Pharisees, Sadducees, and a host of other Jews, godless men. (Acts 2:23) What a difference when the Holy Spirit controlled his soul!

- A believer becomes helpless when the OSN is seated on the command post of his soul. In that position, he has the potential to commit the most heinous sins. We saw this in King David's life when he, a believer, 'a man after God's own heart,' committed adultery and murder. (II Samuel 11:2-4; 12:9) Yes, murder, too! No sin exists that a believer hasn't committed and still remained a believer. Yes, murderers will be in heaven, not because of anything they did or didn't do but because they believed in Christ's work on the Cross.

- When a believer welcomes the OSN into his soul by a simple decision to sin, think contrary to God's Word, or allow evil thoughts to run their course, he has begun his trip down the rugged road of evil deeds. (James 1:14-15) Believers who are frequently led by the nose (deceived) are those who overlook or underestimate the overwhelming power of the OSN!

- Every believer is the gateman of his own soul. He opens the gate to whichever power supply he chooses—the Old Sin Nature or God the Holy Spirit. God has a delightful sense of humor. He elected each human being to be president of his own soul. Consequently, God holds everyone responsible for the choices he makes! The good news is that the Old Sin Nature has to have our permission before taking a seat at the command post of our souls.

- When a believer commits a sin, the OSN remains in command of his soul until he chooses to apply I John 1:9.

    *If we confess* [acknowledge] *our sins* [to God the Father], *He is faithful and righteous to forgive us our sins and to cleanse* [purify] *us from all unrighteousness* [unknown sins]. (I John 1:9)

    Naming our sins to God the Father is the only solution for ousting the Old Sin Nature from our souls and allowing the Holy Spirit to re-enter our souls, thereby giving God control of the command post.

- The length of time the Holy Spirit lodges in a believer's soul is equal to the believer's level of spiritual growth. Consequently, a mature believer understands the importance of the ministry of the Holy Spirit in his soul more than the baby believer, and he is more consistent in confessing his sins to God the Father, diligently learning Bible doctrine, and successfully applying it. Learning Bible doctrine takes on added significance when we realize we can't confess sins we don't recognize. The Bible is the record book of sins. Because God makes His Word available to anyone who wants it, we have no legitimate excuse for not recognizing and avoiding sin.

- God classifies any work that a believer performs when the Holy Spirit is not in command of his soul as "wood, hay, and straw," devoid of rewards both in time and eternity. (I Corinthians 3:12-15)
- Therefore, God's commands us,

  *Do not grieve the Holy Spirit...* (Ephesians 4:30a)

  *Do not quench the* [Holy] *Spirit....* (I Thessalonians 5:19a)

  *Be careful how you walk* [live your spiritual life], *not as unwise men but as wise* ... (Ephesians 5:15)

  *Make the most of your time* [don't consciously expel the Holy Spirit from your soul through sin] *because the days are evil.* (Ephesians 5:16)

  *Do not give the devil an opportunity* [by giving the OSN access to your soul]... (Ephesians 4:27)

  *Keep on being filled with the* [Holy] *Spirit.* (Ephesians 5:18b)
- This spiritual warfare we participate in demands spiritual power! That power comes only through the filling of the Holy Spirit and the Bible doctrine we accumulate in our souls.

## THE WORD OF HIS GRACE

No believer can ever develop grace-orientation apart from acquiring an arsenal of accurate Bible doctrine in his soul. To achieve this, the believer has to make the perception of Bible doctrine (learning with concentration) his number one priority.

Sadly, many believers get tangled in the details of life at the expense of learning God's Word. Such people may say, "When things improve, I will spend more time learning doctrine." Things will NEVER improve until your rapport with your heavenly Father is unshakable! (Joshua 1:8)

Again, perception of Bible doctrine is never the end in glorifying God. Instead, the inventory of doctrine in our souls avails us the opportunity to think divine viewpoint. When we think divine viewpoint, we are applying the divine principles we have learned. We are glorifying God in the only possible way—by applying His Word!

God, in His infinite grace, provided us with His thoughts in writing. We don't deserve to know His thoughts. He graces us out!

## THE MECHANICS OF APPLYING DOCTRINE

The consistent, correct application of God's Word is at the core of successful spiritual warfare. The application mechanism measures whether a believer is legalistic or grace-oriented, whether he is advancing to the high ground of spiritual maturity or retrogressing, becoming a casualty of spiritual conflict. Application of Bible doctrine measures the level of our spiritual growth.

May I pause to underscore a very important fact: Application of Bible doctrine is the most difficult responsibility in our spiritual lives. But can we successfully apply doctrine to our lives on a regular basis? Yes. Can we do it on our own? No chance! The Scripture states clearly that every believer is responsible for learning and applying Bible doctrine on a consistent basis. A believer can have a reservoir of doctrine in his soul, but if he fails to apply it, the doctrines do not benefit him at all.

Many believers have asked, "How can I apply Bible doctrine?" We need to realize one basic point: Application of Bible doctrine varies with individuals and their circumstances. With this in mind, we can now develop a general mechanism for the application of God's Truth:

- THE FILLING OF THE HOLY SPIRIT: The filling of the Holy Spirit is nothing more than God the Holy Spirit taking hold of the command post of the soul. Only when He resides in our souls can we glorify God. He can't be in our souls when we have unconfessed sin in them. We must acknowledge our sins to God the Father before the Holy Spirit can fill and empower us.

- THE DESIRE TO APPLY DOCTRINE: Desire is a key factor in the execution of the unique plan of God. Action is usually a by-product of desire; therefore, our Heavenly Father judges our souls before he judges our actions. The prophet Samuel told us,

  *God sees not as man sees, for man looks at the outward appearance, but the Lord looks at the heart* [soul]. (I Samuel 16:7)

  King Solomon wrote,

  *For as he* [any man] *thinks within himself* [in his soul], *so he is.* (Proverbs 23:7)

  And the Lord echoed,

  *"You shall not commit adultery... everyone who looks at a woman with lust* [a desire to be with her or him] *has committed adultery with her in his heart* [soul]." (Matthew 5:27b-28)

  So when a believer is faced with a test, the issue is, what does he desire? To follow his own desires or God's?

- SPIRITUAL TESTING: The believer faces many types of tests. Suppose he is face-to-face with an obnoxious fellow believer who has ridiculed, maligned and abused him in every cruel way. If the victim of this unfair treatment is grace-oriented, he will turn to the doctrine in his soul and realize that getting even with his enemy or responding in a similar way will not glorify God. Therefore, he *desires* to use this opportunity to glorify God by treating his antagonist with kindness and virtue love.

- THE ENABLING POWER OF THE HOLY SPIRIT: When a believer sends the signal that he desires to glorify God, the Holy Spirit responds by providing him virtue love from the doctrine in his soul, a love he cannot produce on his own. (Galatians 5:22) Then, by the same enabling power, the believer reaches into the reservoir of Bible doctrine in his soul and concentrates on God's Word resident there. For example, he may remember *"Never take your own revenge."* (Romans 12:19a) *"Love your enemies, and pray for those who persecute you."* (Matthew 5:44) As his desire to glorify God intensifies, he becomes motivated to pray for the offending individual, using the same power of the Holy Spirit. In the end, the Holy Spirit produces the *agape* love the believer needs to apply to his enemy and the peace which surpasses human comprehension that engulfs his soul. That's grace in action!

Now, you see why you should never take any credit for your spiritual victories. All credit belongs to the Father, His Spirit, and the Word of His grace!

# CHAPTER ELEVEN
## FINAL THOUGHTS

No question about it, the apostle Paul was a monumental testimony to God's grace! He appropriated divine grace beyond measure and reflected God's grace-orientation to the maximum! Grace was the focal point of his thinking and communication, and so we read these words from Paul,

- *To all who are beloved of God... called as saints: Grace to you....* (Romans 1:7)
- *... For you are not under law, but under grace.* (Romans 6:14)
- *... you have heard of the stewardship* [dispensation] *of God's grace which was given to me* ['the very least of all saints' (Ephesians 3:8)] *for you.* (Ephesians 3:2)
- *In Him, we have redemption through His blood, the forgiveness of our trespasses, according to the riches of His grace.* (Ephesians 1:7)
- *In order that in the ages to come He might show the surpassing riches of His grace in kindness toward us in Christ Jesus.* (Ephesians 2:7).
- *For through the grace given to me I say to every man among you not to think more highly of himself than he ought to think....* (Romans 12:3).
- *Grace be with all of those who love our Lord Jesus Christ with incorruptible* [unquenchable] *love.* (Ephesians 6:24)
- *And now I commend you to God and to the Word of His grace, which is able to build you up and to give you the inheritance among all those who are sanctified.* (Acts 20:32)

Paul began his first epistle with "*grace to you, and peace from God our Father, and the Lord Jesus Christ*" (Galatians 1:3) and ended—in a pastoral epistle to Timothy—"*grace be with you.*" (II Timothy 4:22)

What a life! And what a challenge for us!!

The question that arises is this: If your spiritual life were brought to a screeching halt today and you were face-to-face with the Lord would He say to you, "Well done, good and faithful servant—a trophy of God's grace?" I ponder this issue throughout each day, and you should do likewise.

*Now to Him who is able to keep you from stumbling* [losing your salvation], *and to make you stand in the presence of His glory, blameless* [with no accusation against you] *with great joy, to the only God our Savior, through Jesus Christ our Lord, be glory, majesty, dominion, and authority before all time and now and forever. Amen.* (Jude 1:24-25)

# Publications Available Free of Charge:

*Riding the Death Train*

*Eternal Security of the Believer*

*Comfort in Suffering*

*God's Plan after Salvation*

*Biblical Doctrine of Salvation*

*Focus on Christian Marriage*

*Overview of God's Grace*

*Paul, a Trophy of God's Grace*

*Joseph, A Pillar of Grace*

*Signs & Wonders* (A Biblical Reply to the Claims of Modern Day Miracle Workers)

*The Spiritual Gift of Tongues* (A Biblical Response to Modern Day Tongues)

*Disaster: God's Warning Bell*


"Grow in the grace and knowledge of
our Lord and Savior Jesus Christ.
To Him be the glory, both now and
to the day of eternity. Amen."
(2 Peter 3:18)


**To receive this or any publication, please write to:**

**In the U.S.A.**
Grace Evangelistic Ministries
P.O. Box 111999
Nashville, TN 37222
U.S.A.

**In Africa:**
Grace Evangelistic Ministries
P.O. Box 583
Post Code 930001
Jos, Plateau State
NIGERIA


www.GEMworldwide.org

# Financial Policy

Grace Evangelistic Ministries does not solicit funding. We believe that God in His grace will continue to meet our financial needs as they arise.

We do not charge for our books or audiotapes. We never request any money. Anyone, regardless of financial status, desiring to receive our books, tapes, or other spiritual materials can receive them at absolutely no cost!

When gratitude for the Word of God, the source of true giving, and understanding of the need to reach unsaved souls worldwide with the simple grace gospel and then sound Bible teaching motivate you to contribute, you have the privilege of giving and sharing in the dissemination of the Word of God.

Grace Evangelistic Ministries is exclusively a grace ministry.

# *Notes*

# *Notes*

# *Notes*

*Notes*

# *Notes*

# *Notes*